Frank Richard Stockton, William Randolph Hearst

The Clocks of Rondaine, and other Stories

Frank Richard Stockton, William Randolph Hearst

The Clocks of Rondaine, and other Stories

ISBN/EAN: 9783743305342

Manufactured in Europe, USA, Canada, Australia, Japa

Cover: Foto ©ninafisch / pixelio.de

Manufactured and distributed by brebook publishing software (www.brebook.com)

Frank Richard Stockton, William Randolph Hearst

The Clocks of Rondaine, and other Stories

CONTENTS.

The Clocks of Roundaine . . . . Page	1
The Curious History of a Message . . . . "	24
A Fortunate Opening . . . . "	43
The Christmas Truants . . . . "	75
The Tricycle of the Future . . . . "	92
The Accommodating Circumstance . . . . "	108
The Great Show in Kobol-land . . . . "	129

LIST OF ILLUSTRATIONS.

"So many things stop at night—such as the day itself—that I think you ought to pardon my poor clock" . . . . *Frontispiece*	
Over the roofs of Rondaine . . . . Page	3
"I don't like him as much as I used to," said Arla . . . . . "	8
Arla and the sacristan . . . . "	9
At the telephone . . . . "	24
Elinor and Maud . . . . "	27
The professor wished to find out just how the accident had happened "	32
The bird began circling around the room . . . . "	38
"The Gulf Stream goes to England, doesn't it? Do you suppose it will drift us as far as that?" . . . . "	57
"I cut all the ropes that confined the sail" . . . . "	64
"Up to the pilot-house we rushed, and we both took hold of the great wheel" . . . . "	67
They were marched away to the robbers' cave . . . . "	79
Fred's ideal tricycle of the future . . . . "	99
"A unicycle!" exclaimed Puffy; "what is that?" . . . . . "	107
"You are the noblest man," said Litza . . . "	125

LIST OF ILLUSTRATIONS.

The twin kings . . . . Page	130
"Graglick, measure my grin" . . . . "	134
The journey to Kobol-land . . . . "	137
All fairyland was there . . . . "	139
Gromline and his bean . . . . "	146
Duel between the king and the unicorn . . . . "	161
Prince Atlo takes a ride with the griffin . . . . "	165
The judges of the games . . . . "	167
Athletes at the games . . . . "	170

THE CLOCKS OF RONDAINE.

CENTURIES ago, there stood on the banks of a river a little town called Rondaine. The river was a long and winding stream which ran through different countries, and was sometimes narrow and swift, and sometimes broad and placid; sometimes hurrying through mountain passes, and again meandering quietly through fertile plains; in some places of a blue color and almost transparent, and in others of a dark and sombre hue; and so it changed until it threw itself into a warm, far-spreading sea.

But it was quite otherwise with the little town. As far back as anybody could remember, it had always been the same that it was at the time of our story; and the people who lived there could see no reason to suppose that it would ever be different from what it was then. It was a pleasant little town, its citizens were very happy; and why there should be any change in it, the most astute old man in all Rondaine could not have told you.

If Rondaine had been famed for anything at all, it would have been for the number of its clocks. It had many churches, some little ones in dark side streets, and some larger ones in wider thoroughfares, besides here and there a very good-sized church fronting on a park or open square; and in the steeple of each of these churches there was a clock. There were town buildings, very old ones, which stood upon the great central square. Each of these had a tower, and in each tower was a clock. Then there were clocks at street corners, and two clocks in the market-place, and clocks over shop doors, a clock at each end of the bridge, and several large clocks a little way out of town. Many of these clocks were fashioned in some quaint and curious way. In one of the largest a stone man came out and struck the hours with a stone hammer, while a stone woman struck the half hours with a stone broom; and in another an iron donkey kicked the hours on a bell behind him. It would be impossible to tell all the odd ways in which the clocks of Rondaine struck; but in one respect they were alike: they all did strike. The good people of the town would not have tolerated a clock which did not strike.

It was very interesting to lie awake in the night and hear the clocks of Rondaine strike. First would come a faint striking from one of the churches in the by-streets, a modest sound, as if the clock was not sure whether it was too early or not; then from another quarter would be heard a more confident clock striking the hour clearly and distinctly. When they were quite ready, but not a moment before, the seven bells of the large church on the square would chime the hour; after which, at a respectful interval of time, the other church clocks of the town would strike. After the lapse of three or four minutes, the sound of all these bells seemed to wake up the stone man in the tower of the town building, and he struck the hour with his hammer. When this had been done, the other municipal clocks felt at liberty to strike, and they did so. And when every sound had died away, so that he would be certain to be heard if there was any one awake to hear, it would be very likely that the iron donkey would kick out the hour on his bell. But there were times when he kicked before any of the clocks began to strike. One by one the clocks on the street corners struck, the uptown ones first, and afterward those near the river.

These were followed by the two clocks on the bridge, the one at the country end waiting until it was quite sure that the one at the town end had finished. Somewhat later would be heard the clock of Vougereau, an old country house in the suburbs. This clock, a very large one, was on the top of a great square stone tower, and from its age it had acquired a habit of deliberation; and when it began to strike people were very apt to think that it was one o'clock, until after a considerable interval another stroke would assure them that it was later or earlier than that, and if they really wanted to know what hour the old clock was striking they must give themselves time enough to listen until they were entirely certain that it had finished.

The very last clock to strike in Rondaine was one belonging to a little old lady with white hair, who lived in a little white house in one of the prettiest and cleanest streets in the town. Her clock was in a little white tower at the corner of her house, and was the only strictly private clock which was in the habit of making itself publicly heard. Long after every other clock had struck, and when there was every reason to believe that for a considerable time nothing but half-hours would be heard in Rondaine, the old lady's clock would strike quickly and decisively, and with a confident tone, as if it knew it was right, and wished everybody to know that it knew.

In an unpretentious house which stood on a corner of two of the smaller streets in the town lived a young girl named Arla. For a year or more Arla had been in the habit of waking up very early in the morning, sometimes long before daylight, and it had become a habit with her to lie and listen to the clocks. Her room was at the top of the house, and one of its windows opened to the west and another to the south, so that sounds entered from different quarters. Arla liked to leave these windows open so that the sounds of the clocks might come in.

Arla knew every clock by its tone, and she always made it a point to lie awake until she was positively sure that the last stroke of the clock at Vougereau had sounded; but it often happened that sleep overcame her before she heard the clock of the little old lady with white hair. It was so very long to wait for that!

It was not because she wanted to know the hour that Arla used to lie and listen to the clocks. She had a little clock of her own, which stood in her room, and on which she depended for correct information regarding the time of day or night. This little clock, which had been given to her when she was a small girl, not only struck the hours and half-hours and quarter-hours, but there was attached to it a very pretty piece of mechanism which also indicated the time. On the front of the clock, just below the dial, was a sprig of a rosebush beautifully made of metal, and on this, just after the hour had sounded, there was a large green bud; at a quarter past the hour this bud opened a little, so that the red petals could be seen; fifteen minutes later it was a half-blown rose, and at a quarter of an hour more it was nearly full blown; just before the hour the rose opened to its fullest extent, and so remained until the clock had finished striking, when it immediately shut up into a great green bud. This clock was a great delight to Arla; for not only was it a very pleasant thing to watch the unfolding of the rose, but it was a continual satisfaction to her to think that her little clock always told her exactly what time it was, no matter what the other clocks of Rondaine might say.

Arla's father and mother were thrifty, industrious people, who were very fond of their daughter. They not only taught her how to employ herself usefully, but insisted that she should take the recreation and exercise that a young girl ought to have. All day she was so occupied with work or play that she had little opportunity of thinking for herself; but even if they had considered the matter, this fact would not have troubled her parents, as they looked upon Arla as entirely too young for that sort of thing. In the very early morning, however, listening to the clocks of Rondaine or waiting for them, Arla did a great deal of thinking; and it so happened, on the morning of the day before Christmas, when the stars were bright and the air frosty, and every outside sound very clear and distinct, that Arla began to think of something which had never entered her mind before.

"How in the world," she said to herself, "do the people of

Rondaine know when it is really Christmas? Christmas begins as soon as it is twelve o'clock on Christmas Eve; but as some of the people depend for the time upon one clock and some upon others, a great many of them cannot truly know when Christmas Day has really begun. Even some of the church clocks make people think that Christmas has come, when in reality it is yet the day before. And not one of them strikes at the right time! As for that iron donkey, I believe he kicks whenever he feels like it. And yet there are people who go by him! I know this, for they have told me so. But the little old lady with white hair is worse off than anybody else. Christmas must always come ever so long before she knows it."

With these important thoughts on her mind, Arla could not go to sleep again. She heard all the clocks strike, and lay awake until her own little clock told her that she ought to get up. During this time she had made up her mind what she should do. There was yet one day before Christmas; and if the people of the town could be made to see in what a deplorable condition they were on account of the difference in their clocks, they might have time to rectify the matter so that all the clocks should strike the correct hour, and everybody should know exactly when Christmas Day began. She was sure that the citizens had never given this matter proper consideration; and it was quite natural that such should be the case, for it was not every one who was in the habit of lying awake in the very early morning; and in the daytime, with all the out-door noises, one could not hear all the clocks strike in Rondaine. Arla, therefore, thought that a great deal depended upon her, who knew exactly how this matter stood.

When she went down to breakfast she asked permission of her mother to take a day's holiday. As she was a good girl, and never neglected either her lessons or her tasks, her mother was quite willing to give her the day before Christmas in which she could do as she pleased, and she did not think it necessary to ask if she intended to spend it in any particular way. The day was cool, but the sun shone brightly and the air was pleasant. In the country around about Rondaine Christmas-time was not a very cold season. Arla put on a warm jacket and a pretty blue hood, and started out gayly to attend to the business in hand. Everybody in Rondaine knew her father and mother, and a great many of them knew her, so there was no reason why she should be afraid to go where she chose. In one hand she carried a small covered basket in which she had placed her rose clock. The works of this little clock were regulated by a balance-wheel, like those of a watch, and therefore it could be carried about without stopping it.

The first place she visited was the church at which she and her parents always attended service. It was a small building in a little square at the bottom of a hill, and, to reach it, one had to go down a long flight of stone steps. When she entered the dimly lighted church, Arla soon saw the sacristan, a pleasant-faced little old man whom she knew very well.

"Good-morning, sir," said she. "Do you take care of the church clock?"

The sacristan was sweeping the stone pavements of the church, just inside the door. He stopped and leaned upon his broom. "Yes, my little friend," he said, "I take care of everything here except the souls of the people."

"Well, then," said Arla, "I think you ought to know that your clock is eleven minutes too fast. I came here to tell you that, so that you might change it, and make it strike properly."

The sacristan's eyes began to twinkle. He was a man of merry mood. "That is very good of you, little Arla; very good indeed."

And, now that we are about it, isn't there something else you would like to change? What do you say to having these stone pillars put to one side, so that they may be out of the way of the people when they come in? Or those great beams in the roof— they might be turned over, and perhaps we might find that the upper side would look fresher than this lower part, which is somewhat time-stained, as you see? Or, for the matter of that, what do you say to having our clock-tower taken down and set out there in the square before the church door? Then short-sighted people could see the time much better, don't you think? Now tell me, shall we do all these things together, wise little friend?"

A tear or two came into Arla's eyes, but she made no answer.

"Good-morning, sir," she said, and went away.

"I DON'T LIKE HIM AS MUCH AS I USED TO,"
SAID ARLA.

"I suppose," she said to herself as she ran up the stone steps, "that he thought it would be too much trouble to climb to the top of the tower to set the clock right. But that was no reason why he should make fun of me. I don't like him as much as I used to."

The next church to which Arla went was a large one, and it was some time before she could find the sacristan. At last she

ARLA AND THE SACRISTAN.

saw him in a side chapel at the upper end of the church, engaged in dusting some old books. He was a large man, with a red face, and he turned around quickly, with a stern expression, as she entered.

"Please, sir," said Arla, "I came to tell you that your church clock is wrong. It strikes from four to six minutes before it ought to; sometimes the one and sometimes the other. It should be changed so that it will be sure to strike at the right time."

The face of the sacristan grew redder and twitched visibly at her remark.

"Do you know what I wish?" he almost shouted in reply.

"No, sir," answered Arla.

"I wish," he said, "that you were a boy, so that I might take you by the collar and soundly cuff your ears, for coming here to insult an officer of the church in the midst of his duties! But, as you are a girl, I can only tell you to go away from here as rapidly and as quietly as you can, or I shall have to put you in the hands of the ecclesiastical authorities!"

Arla was truly frightened, and although she did not run—for she knew that would not be proper in a church—she walked as fast as she could into the outer air.

"What a bad man," she then said to herself, "to be employed in a church! It surely is not known what sort of person he is, or he would not be allowed to stay there a day!"

Arla thought she would not go to any more churches at present, for she did not know what sort of sacristans she might find in them.

"When the other clocks in the town all strike properly," she thought, "it is most likely they will see for themselves that their clocks are wrong, and they will have them changed."

She now made her way to the great square of the town, and

entered the building at the top of which stood the stone man with his hammer. She found the concierge, or doorkeeper, in a little room by the side of the entrance. She knew where to go, for she had been there with her mother to ask permission to go up and see the stone man strike the hour with his hammer, and the stone woman strike the half-hour with her broom.

The concierge was a grave, middle-aged man with spectacles; and, remembering what had just happened, Arla thought she would be careful how she spoke to him.

"If you please, sir," she said, with a courtesy, "I should like to say something to you. And I hope you will not be offended when I tell you that your clock is not quite right. Your stone man and your stone woman are both too slow; they sometimes strike as much as seven minutes after they ought to strike."

The grave, middle-aged man looked steadily at her through his spectacles.

"I thought," continued Arla, "that if this should be made known to you, you would have the works of the stone man and the stone woman altered so that they might strike at the right time. They can be heard so far, you know, that it is very necessary they should not make mistakes."

"Child," said the man, with his spectacles still steadily fixed on her, "for one hundred and fifty-seven years the open tower on this building has stood there. For one hundred and fifty-seven years the thunder and the lightning in time of storm have roared and flashed around it, and the sun in time of fair weather has shone upon it. In that century and a half and seven years men and women have lived and have died, and their children and their grandchildren and their great-grandchildren, and even the children of these, have lived and died after them. Kings and queens have passed away, one after another; and all things living have grown old and died, one generation after another, many times. And yet, through all these years, that stone man and that stone woman have stood there, and in storm and in fair weather, by daylight or in the darkness of night, they have struck the hours and the half-hours. Of all things that one hundred and fifty-seven years ago were able to lift an arm to strike, they alone are left. And now you, a child of thirteen, or perhaps fourteen years, come to me and ask me to change that which has not been changed for a century and a half and seven years!"

Arla could answer nothing with those spectacles fixed upon her. They seemed to glare more and more as she looked at them. "Good-morning, sir," she said, dropping a courtesy as she moved backward toward the door. Reaching it, she turned and hurried into the street.

"If those stone people," she thought, "have not been altered in all these years, it is likely they would now be striking two or three hours out of the way! But I don't know. If they kept on going slow for more than a century, they must have come around to the right hour sometimes. But they will have to strike ever and ever so much longer before they come around there again!"

Arla now walked on until she came to a street corner where a cobbler had a little shop. In the angle of the wall of the house, at the height of the second story, was a clock. This cobbler did not like the confined air and poor light of his shop, and whenever the weather allowed he always worked outside on the sidewalk. To-day, although it was winter, the sun shone brightly on this side of the street, and he had put his bench outside, close to his door, and was sitting there, hard at work. When Arla stopped before him he looked up and said, cheerfully:

"Good-morning, Mistress Arla. Do you want them half-soled, or heeled, or a patch put on the toes?"

"My shoes do not need mending," said Arla. "I came to ask you if you could tell me who has charge of the clock at this corner?"

"I can easily do that," he said, "for I am the man. I am paid by the year, for winding it up and keeping it in order, as much as I should get for putting the soles, heels, tops, linings, and buckles on a pair of shoes."

"Which means making them out and out," said Arla.

"You are right," said he, "and the pay is not great; but if it were larger, more people might want it and I might lose it; and if it were less, how could I afford to do it at all? So I am satisfied."

"But you ought not to be entirely satisfied," said Arla, "for the clock does not keep good time. I know when it is striking, for it has a very jangling sound, and it is the most irregular clock in Rondaine. Sometimes it strikes as much as twenty-five minutes after the hour, and very often it does not strike at all."

The cobbler looked up at her with a smile. "I am sorry," he said, "that it has a jangling stroke, but the fashioning of clocks is not my trade, and I could not mend its sound with awl, hammer, or waxed-end. But it seems to me, my good maiden, that you never mended a pair of shoes."

"No, indeed!" said Arla; "I should do that even worse than you would make clocks."

"Never having mended shoes, then," said the cobbler, "you do not know what a grievous thing it is to have twelve o'clock, or six o'clock, or any other hour, in fact, come before you are ready for it. Now, I don't mind telling you, because I know you are too good to spoil the trade of a hard-working cobbler—and shoemaker too, whenever he gets the chance to be one—that when I have promised a customer that he shall have his shoes or his boots at a certain time of day, and that time is drawing near, and the end of the job is still somewhat distant, then do I skip up the stairway and set back the hands of the clock according to the work that has to be done. And when my customer comes I look up to the clock-face and I say to him, 'Glad to see you!' and then he will look up at the clock and will say, 'Yes, I am a little too soon;' and then, as likely as not, he will sit down on the door-step here by me and talk entertainingly; and it may happen that he will sit there without grumbling for many minutes after the clock has pointed out the hour at which the shoes were promised. Sometimes, when I have been much belated in beginning a job, I stop the clock altogether, for you can well see for yourself that it would not do to have it strike eleven when it is truly twelve. And so, if my man be willing to sit down, and our talk be very entertaining, the clock being above him where he cannot see it without stepping outward from the house, he may not notice that it is stopped. This expedient once served me very well, for an old gentleman, over-testy and over-punctual, once came to me for his shoes, and looking up at the clock, which I had prepared for him, exclaimed, 'Bless me! I am much too early!' And he sat down by me for three-quarters of an hour, in which time I persuaded him that his shoes were far too much worn to be worth mending any more, and that he should have a new pair, which, afterward, I made."

"I do not believe it is right for you to do that," said Arla; "but even if you think so, there is no reason why your clock should go wrong at night, when so many people can hear it because of the stillness."

"Ah, me!" said the cobbler, "I do not object to the clock being as right as you please in the night; but when my day's work is done, I so desire to go home to my supper that I often forget to put the clock right, or to set it going if it is stopped. But so many things stop at night—such as the day itself—and so many things then go wrong—such as the ways of evil-minded people—that I think you truly ought to pardon my poor clock."

"Then you will not consent," said Arla, "to make it go right?"

"I will do that with all cheerfulness," answered the cobbler, pulling out a pair of waxed-ends with a great jerk, "as soon as I can make myself go right. The most important thing should always be done first; and, surely, I am more important than a clock!" And he smiled with great good-humor.

Arla knew that it would be of no use to stand there any longer and talk with this cobbler. Turning to go, she said:

"When I bring you shoes to mend, you shall finish them by my clock, and not by yours."

"That will I, my good little Arla," said the cobbler, heartily. "They shall be finished by any clock in town, and five minutes before the hour, or no payment."

Arla now walked on until she came to the bridge over the river. It was a long, covered structure, and by the entrance sat the bridge-keeper.

"Do you know, sir," said she, "that the clock at this end of your bridge does not keep the same time as the one at the other end? They are not so very different, but I have noticed that this one is always done striking at least two minutes before the other begins."

The bridge-keeper looked at her with one eye, which was all he had.

"You are as wrong as anybody can be," said he. "I do not say anything about the striking, because my ears are not now good enough to hear the clock at the other end when I am near this one; but I know they both keep the same time. I have often looked at this clock and have then walked to the other end of the bridge, and have found that the clock there was exactly like it."

Arla looked at the poor old man, whose legs were warmly swaddled on account of his rheumatism, and said:

"But it must take you a good while to walk to the other end of the bridge."

"Out upon you!" cried the bridge-keeper. "I am not so old as that yet! I can walk there in no time!"

Arla now crossed the bridge and went a short distance along a country road until she came to the great stone house known as Vougereau. This belonged to a rich family who seldom came there, and the place was in charge of an elderly man who was the brother of Arla's mother. When his niece was shown into a room on the ground floor, which served for his parlor and his office, he was very glad to see her; and while Arla was having something to eat and drink after her walk, the two had a pleasant chat.

"I came this time, Uncle Anton," she said, "not only to see you, but to tell you that the great clock in your tower does not keep good time."

Uncle Anton looked at her a little surprised.

"How do you know that, my dear?" he said.

Then Arla told him how she had lain awake in the early morning, and had heard the striking of the different clocks. "If you wish to make it right," said she, "I can give you the proper time, for I have brought my own little clock with me."

She was about to take her rose-clock out of her basket, when her uncle motioned to her not to do so.

"Let me tell you something," said he. "The altering of the time of day, which you speak of so lightly, is a very serious matter, which should be considered with all gravity. If you set back a clock, even as little as ten minutes, you add that much to the time that has passed. The hour which has just gone by has been made seventy minutes long. Now, no human being has the right to add anything to the past, nor to make hours longer than they were originally made. And, on the other hand, if you set a clock forward even so little as ten minutes, you take away that much from the future, and you make the coming hour only fifty minutes long. Now, no human being has a right to take anything away from the future, or to make the hours shorter than they were originally intended to be. I desire, my dear niece, that you will earnestly think over what I have said, and I am sure that you will then see for yourself how unwise and even culpable it would be to trifle with the length of the hours which make up our day. And now, Arla, let us talk of other things."

And so they talked of other things until Arla thought it was time to go. She saw there was something wrong in her uncle's reasoning, although she could not tell exactly what it was, and thinking about it, she slowly returned to the town. As she approached the house of the little old lady with white hair, she concluded to stop and speak to her about her clock. "She will surely be willing to alter that," said Arla, "for it is so very much out of the way."

The old lady knew who Arla was, and received her very kindly; but when she heard why the young girl had come to her, she flew into a passion.

"Never, since I was born," she said, "have I been spoken to like this! My great-grandfather lived in this house before me; that clock was good enough for him! My grandfather lived in this house before me; that clock was good enough for him! My father and mother lived in this house before me; that clock was good enough for them! I was born in this house, have always lived in it, and expect to die in it; that clock is good enough for me! I heard its strokes when I was but a little child, I hope to hear them at my last hour; and sooner than raise my hand against the clock of my ancestors, and the clock of my whole life, I would cut off that hand!"

Some tears came into Arla's eyes; she was a little frightened. "I hope you will pardon me, good madam," she said, "for, truly, I did not wish to offend you. Nor did I think that your clock is not a good one. I only meant that you should make it better; it is nearly an hour out of the way."

The sight of Arla's tears cooled the anger of the little old lady with white hair. "Child," she said, "you do not know what you are talking about, and I forgive you. But remember this: never ask persons as old as I am to alter the principles which have always made clear to them what they should do, or the clocks which have always told them when they should do it."

And, kissing Arla, she bade her good-by.

"Principles may last a great while without altering," thought Arla, as she went away, "but I am sure it is very different with clocks."

The poor girl now felt a good deal discouraged.

"People don't seem to care whether their clocks are right or not," she said to herself, "and if they don't care, I am sure it is of no use for me to tell them about it. If even one clock could be made to go properly, it might help to make the people of Rondaine care to know exactly what time it is. Now, there is that iron donkey. If he would but kick at the right hour it would be an excellent thing, for he kicks so hard that he is heard all over the town."

Determined to make this one more effort, Arla walked quickly to the town-building, at the top of which was the clock with the iron donkey. This building was a sort of museum; it had a great many curious things in it, and it was in charge of a very ingenious man, who was learned and skilful in various ways.

When Arla had informed the superintendent of the museum why she had come to him, he did not laugh at her nor did he get angry. He was accustomed to giving earnest consideration to matters of this sort, and he listened attentively to all that Arla had to say.

"You must know," he said, "that our iron donkey is a very complicated piece of mechanism. Not only must he kick out the hours, but five minutes before doing so he must turn his head around and look at the bell behind him; and then, when he has done kicking, he must put his head back into its former position. All this action requires a great many wheels and cogs and springs and levers, and these cannot be made to move with absolute regularity. When it is cold, some of his works contract; and when it is warm, they expand; and there are other reasons why he is very likely to lose or gain time. At noon on every bright day I set him right, being able to get the correct time from a sun-dial which stands in the courtyard. But his works—which I am sorry to say are not well made—are sure to get a great deal out of the way before I set him again."

"Then, if there are several cloudy or rainy days together, he goes very wrong indeed," said Arla.

"Yes, he truly does," replied the superintendent, "and I am sorry for it. But there is no way to remedy his irregularities except for me to make him all over again at my own expense, and that is something I cannot afford to do. The clock belongs to the town, and I am sure the citizens will not be willing to spend the money necessary for a new donkey-clock; for, so far as I know, every person but yourself is perfectly satisfied with this one."

"I suppose so," said Arla, with a sigh; "but it really is a great pity that every striking-clock in Rondaine should be wrong!"

"But how do you know they are all wrong?" asked the superintendent.

"Oh, that is easy enough," said Arla. "When I lie awake in the early morning, when all else is very still, I listen to their striking, and then I look at my own rose-clock to see what time it really is."

"Your rose-clock?" said the superintendent.

"This is it," said Arla, opening her basket and taking out her little clock.

The superintendent took it into his hands and looked at it attentively, both outside and inside. And then, still holding it, he stepped out into the courtyard. When in a few moments he returned, he said:

"I have compared your clock with my sun-dial, and find that it is ten minutes slow. I also see that, like the donkey-clock, its works are not adjusted in such a way as to be unaffected by heat and cold."

"My—clock—ten—minutes—slow!" exclaimed Arla, with wide-open eyes.

"Yes," said the superintendent, "that is the case to-day, and on some days it is, probably, a great deal too fast. Such a clock as this—which is a very ingenious and beautiful one—ought frequently to be compared with a sun-dial or other correct time-keeper, and set to the proper hour. I see it requires a peculiar key with which to set it. Have you brought this with you?"

"No, sir," said Arla; "I did not suppose it would be needed."

"Well, then," said the superintendent, "you can set it forward ten minutes when you reach home; and if to-morrow morning you compare the other clocks with it, I think you will find that not all of them are wrong."

Arla sat quiet for a moment, and then she said: "I think I shall not care any more to compare the clocks of Rondaine with my little rose-clock. If the people are satisfied with their own clocks, whether they are fast or slow, and do not desire to know exactly when Christmas Day begins, I can do nobody any good by listening to the different strikings and then looking at my own little clock, with a night-lamp by it."

"Especially," said the superintendent, with a smile, "when you are not sure that your rose-clock is right. But if you will bring here your little clock and your key on any day when the sun is shining, I will set it to the time shadowed on the sun-dial, or show you how to do it yourself."

"Thank you very much," said Arla, and she took her leave.

As she walked home, she lifted the lid of her basket and looked at her little rose-clock. "To think of it!" she said. "That you should be sometimes too fast and sometimes too slow! And, worse than that, to think that some of the other clocks have been right and you have been wrong! But I do not feel like altering you to-day. If you go fast sometimes, and slow sometimes, you must be right sometimes, and one of these days, when I take you to be compared with the sun-dial, perhaps you will not have to be altered so much."

Arla went to bed that night quite tired with her long walks, and when she awoke it was broad daylight. "I do not know," she said to herself, "exactly when Christmas began, but I am very sure that the happy day is here."

"Do you lie awake in the morning as much as you used to?" asked Arla's mother, a few weeks after the Christmas holidays.

"No, mother, dear," said Arla; "I now sleep with one of my

windows shut, and I am no longer awakened by that chilly feeling which used to come to me in the early morning, when I would draw the bed-covers close about me and think how wrong were the clocks of Rondaine."

And the little rose-clock never went to be compared with the sun-dial. "Perhaps you are right now," Arla would say to her clock each day when the sun shone, "and I will not take you until some time when I feel very sure that you are wrong."

THE CURIOUS HISTORY OF A MESSAGE.

THE winter in which the events of this history occurred opened very disagreeably. The cold was not intense nor the snows deep, but it was a sloppy, sleety, slippery December, in which one could expect neither good ice nor good sleighing.

The probabilities of an unseasonable Christmas were very much discussed by the members of a family named Kinton, who lived in a country house about thirty miles from New York. Mrs. Kinton was a widow, and her family was made up of herself and three daughters, whose ages ranged from seventeen to six. Her brother, Mr. Rodney Carr, was very often with them, but his presence was not at all to be depended upon.

The two older girls, Elinor and Maud, were generally ready to enjoy Christmas in any weather and in any place; but this year the prospect of a Christmas at home appeared extremely distasteful to them, on account of a certain other prospect that had been held out to them by their Uncle Rodney. This uncle was a generous man, and always glad to promote the pleasure of his nieces; and early in this winter he had made them a half-promise of something which Mrs. Kinton thought he should have said nothing about until he had felt himself able to make a whole promise. He had gone to California upon business; and, before starting, had told Elinor and Maud that, if a certain enterprise proved successful, he would make them a Christmas present of a trip to the Bermudas. This unusual gift had been suggested to him by the fact that the most intimate friends of Elinor and Maud, the two Sanderson girls, who spent their winters in New York, were going with their mother to the Bermudas for their Christmas holidays; and Mrs. Sanderson had told him that she would be very glad if his nieces could go with them.

The state of mind of the Kinton girls can easily be imagined. A Christmas in the Bermudas—two weeks of balmy air, warm sunshine, oranges, bananas, pineapples, roses in the open air! It made them wild to talk about it!

Christmas was coming nearer and nearer, when a letter was received from Uncle Rodney; and he, it appeared, was also coming nearer and nearer. He was on his way from California; and, to the surprise of the Kinton family, he was also on his way to England. The business which took him there, he wrote, was pressing; and as he wished to catch a certain steamer, it would be impossible for him to stop to see his relatives. He had not yet decided the important question of a trip to the Bermudas; but on the way he would make some calculations, and see whether or not he would be able to give them this pleasure, and, as he would pass through Afton, their railroad station, where the train stopped for a few minutes, he would send them his decision by telephone.

The Kinton house, like several other residences in the neighborhood, was connected with the railroad station, about four miles distant, by a telephone wire; and communication in this way was often very useful, especially in bad weather.

At first the girls declared that they would wait for no telephone, but would go to the station and see Uncle Rodney, if it were only for a minute; but on consulting a time-table of the railroad they found that the train on which their uncle would travel would reach Afton very early in the morning; and Mrs. Kinton put a veto upon the proposition to take the long drive at such an unseasonable hour. Consequently there was nothing to do but to wait for the day on which Uncle Rodney had said he would pass through Afton, and be ready at the telephone at the proper time.

On the day after the receipt of this letter there came to the Kinton house a pleasant, little, middle-aged gentleman, who received a hearty welcome from every member of the family. This was Professor Cupper, an old friend and a man of science. It was his custom, whenever he felt like it, to spend a few days with the Kintons. Seasons and weather made no difference to him. Friends were friends at any time of the year; and weather which might be bad for ordinary purposes was often very suitable for scientific investigations.

Of course the professor was soon made acquainted with the exciting state of affairs, in which he immediately took an animated interest. He well knew what winter-time was in the Bermudas. He knew how his dear young friends would enjoy Christmas among the roses and the palmettos; and he talked so enthusiastically about the land of flowers that the girls were filled with a wilder impatience, and even their mother admitted that she was beginning to be nervously anxious to know what Rodney would say. If the girls were to be in the Bermudas before Christmas, it was necessary to know the fact soon, for certain preparations would have to be made. If Rodney were not such a queer sort of fellow, she said, he would have made up his mind days ago, and would have written or telegraphed his decision.

ELINOR AND MAUD.

But this sort of touch-and-go communication suited his fancies exactly.

The eventful morning arrived. Before it was yet light the two girls were up, dressed, and at the telephone. They had no reason to expect the message so soon; but the train might be ahead of time, and Uncle Rodney might have but half a minute in which to say what he had to tell them. On no account must the telephone bell ring without some one being there to give an instant response.

Consequently the Kinton girls, even little Ruth, were at the instrument, where Professor Cupper speedily made his appearance, and not long afterward Mrs. Kinton joined the expectant group.

The moment arrived at which the message could reasonably be expected. All were in a tingle! The moment passed; it became long past. The girls looked aghast at each other! What had happened? Even the ruddy face of the professor seemed to pale a little. He stepped to the instrument and sounded the signal. No answer came. He sounded again and again, with like result. For ten or fifteen minutes he called and rang without response.

"What can possibly be the matter?" cried Elinor. "Is everybody dead or asleep at the station?"

"Not likely," said the professor. "But it is likely that your wire is broken."

At this announcement the girls broke into lamentations. Uncle Rodney must have arrived and departed, and the words which he had undoubtedly spoken into the telephone at the station had been lost! Now, how could they know what their uncle had decided upon? How could they know whether he intended them to go to the Bermudas or not? He was to sail from New York that day, but he had not informed them what steamer he intended to take, and they did not know where to send a telegram. He had asked them to write to him in the care of a banker in London; but if they were to send a letter after him, it would be so long before they could get an answer to it! Even a message by cable would not be much better, for he would not receive it long before he would receive a letter. There was absolutely nothing which they could do.

This mournful conclusion weighed heavily upon the whole family. Even little Ruth, who did not exactly understand the state of affairs, looked as if she were about to cry.

"I should have liked it better," exclaimed Maud, "if Uncle Rodney had told us we could not go; but to hear, after the holidays are over, that we might have gone, would be simply too hard to bear."

"As soon as I have had some breakfast," said the professor, "I will go to the station—if Mrs. Kinton will give me a conveyance—and I will find out what has happened."

"And we will go with you!" cried Elinor and Maud.

After a hasty breakfast the professor and the two girls set out in a sleigh for Afton. The snow was soft and not very deep, and the roadway beneath was rough; but notwithstanding the bumps and jolts, and the occasional blood-curdling gratings of the runners upon bare places, the impatient girls urged George, the driver, to keep his horses on their fastest trot.

When they were about half-way to the station the professor cried out:

"Hi! there it is! The line is broken!"

All looked around and could see plainly enough that the wire had parted near one of the poles, and that part of it was resting on the ground. But it was of no use to stop; they were in a hurry to reach Afton to learn if Uncle Rodney had been there, and if he had left a message.

When they reached the railroad station they found that Mr.
Carr had arrived on time; that he had telephoned to his sister's
house; and that he had gone. The station-master told them that
he had been outside, and had not heard what Mr. Carr had said,
but that he thought it probable, since he had a very short time in
which to say anything, that he had rung the bell, and, without
waiting for an answering ring, had delivered his message.

"That is very likely," said the professor, "for Mr. Carr knew
that his nieces were expecting to hear from him at the moment
the train arrived here, and that they would, therefore, be ready at
their telephone. But as the line was broken, of course the message never reached them."

Very much dispirited, the little party drove home. The girls
had been buoying themselves up with the hope that Uncle Rodney knew that the wire was broken, and had left a message for
them at the station; but, instead of this, he had gone away in the
belief that he had communicated with them, and would, therefore,
do no more. Now they could not expect to hear from him until
he reached England, and it would then be too late. The kindly
nature of the professor was affected by this disappointment of his
young friends; and the thought came to him that, had he been
rich enough, he would himself have made them a present of a
trip to the Bermudas. Even George, the driver, who knew all
about the affair, and was deeply interested in it, wore a doleful
face.

They drove slowly homeward, and when they reached the
place where the wire had been broken the professor asked
George to stop, and he got out to take a look into the condition of affairs. There was no real need that he should do this,
for, of course, he could not repair the damage, and the station-master had promised to attend to that. But he had an investi-

gating mind, and he wished to find out just how the accident had happened.

It was easy enough to see how the wire had been broken. A

THE PROFESSOR WISHED TO FIND OUT JUST HOW THE ACCIDENT HAD HAPPENED.

tall tree stood near the spot, and from this a heavy dead limb had fallen, which must have struck the wire; this had been broken off close to one of the poles, and from the supporting insulator near the top of the pole an end of the wire, an inch or two in length, projected. From looking up at the damaged wire, the professor glanced down the pole, and when his eyes rested upon the ground he saw there, lying on the frozen crust of the snow, a little dead bird, its wings partly outspread.

The professor stepped quickly to the pole, and, stooping, regarded the bird. Then he stood up, stepped back a little and looked up at the broken wire. After which he advanced toward the bird, and looked down at it. From these observations he was called away by the girls, who wished to know what he was looking at.

Without answering, the professor carefully picked up the bird, and returned to the sleigh.

"It is a poor little dead bird!" exclaimed Maud; "a dead, frozen bird!"

"Yes," said the professor, "that is what it is." And, resuming his seat, they moved on.

For the rest of the way the professor did not talk much; and when they reached the house, without taking off his hat, coat, or overshoes, he sat down on a chair in the hall and steadfastly regarded the bird, which lay in his outspread hands.

Mrs. Kinton, with Ruth, came hurrying down-stairs. "Did you discover anything?" she asked.

Maud was about to speak when the professor interrupted. "Yes," he said, delivering his words slowly and with earnestness, "I think I have discovered something. I have reason to believe that the message sent by Rodney Carr is in this bird."

Exclamations of amazement burst from all his hearers. "What do you mean?" cried Mrs. Kinton.

"I will tell you," said the professor. And they all gathered around him, gazing with astonished eyes at the bird which he held. "By a falling limb," he said, "your telephone wire was broken close to the glass insulator on one of the poles, and on the side of the pole nearest this house. At the bottom of the pole, directly under the fracture, I found this dead bird. Now, my theory is this. The limb probably fell during the high wind of last night. The bird, taking an early morning flight, alighted on the broken end of the wire, which projected a little from the pole after the manner of a twig. While settling on this slight perch, and probably fluttering its wings as it took its position, Mr. Carr sent his message along the wire.

"If the end had merely projected into the air, there would have been no circuit, and no message: but the bird's little feet were on the wire, one of his fluttering wings probably touched the pole or the block, a connection with the earth was made, and the message passed into the bird. The little creature was instantly killed, and dropped to the ground, its wings still outspread."

"Do you mean," cried Elinor, "that you believe Uncle Rodney's message is now in that bird?"

"Yes," said the professor, his eyes sparkling as he spoke, "I believe, or, at least, I strongly conjecture, that your uncle's message is now in that curious complication of electric threads which is diffused through the body of a bird, as it is through that of a man, and which is known as the nervous system."

Mrs. Kinton and her eldest daughter were too surprised to say a word, but Maud exclaimed:

"A dead bird with a message in his nervous system is of no good to anybody! Oh, you poor little thing, not only dead, but frozen, if you could but wake up and tell us whether Uncle Rodney said we were to go to the Bermudas or not to go, you would be the dearest and best bird in the world!"

"I have been considering this matter very earnestly," said Professor Cupper, "and I am going to try to get that message out of the bird. If its nervous system is charged with the modulated electric current produced by your uncle's words, I do not see why those modulations should not be transferred to a delicate electrical machine, which should record or repeat the message, faintly perhaps, but with force enough for us to determine its purport."

"If you can do that," said Elinor, "it will be a miracle!"

Mrs. Kinton's mind was in a state of bewilderment. She could not readily put full faith in what the professor had said, and yet science had done so many wonderful things, and the professor himself had done so many wonderful things, that she could not bring herself to entirely doubt him; so she gave up all attempts to comprehend the matter, and went away to attend to her household duties. At any rate, his efforts to get a telephone message out of a bird could hurt nobody, and if he succeeded in interesting and diverting her daughters it would be a positive benefit.

The girls plied the professor with questions, and the more he discussed the subject the more firmly he became persuaded that it would be a crime against science to allow this great and unique opportunity to pass unimproved.

He did not take off his hat and coat at all; but, calling to Mrs. Kinton, he earnestly requested her to send him to the station in time to take the next train to New York. There he would procure the electrical appliances which he needed, and return to her house in the evening, or, at the latest, the next morning.

Of course the professor went to New York, for everybody could see that he must not be thwarted in this most important investigation. He would have taken the bird with him, to try his experiments on it in the city, but apart from the fear that the electrical conditions of the little thing's nervous system might be disturbed by the journey, he was determined that the girls should hear their uncle's message the moment it was reproduced, if, indeed, he should be able to reproduce it at all.

How this message was to be made known, whether by means of a phonograph or a graphophone, or some other electric appliance, the professor did not say. He was going to consult with some scientific brethren, and they would help him to determine what sort of experiments ought to be tried. He would bring back with him the necessary instruments, and perhaps also one or more of his learned friends, for this was a matter in which he was sure all scientific minds would be interested.

The bird whose nervous system, according to Professor Cupper's belief, was charged with the electric message in which Elinor and Maud took so deep an interest, was left with these two girls by the professor, with injunctions to take the best of care of it. Accordingly they carried it into an unused upper room, and there it was gently placed upon a small table; and when they went out they carefully closed the door, in order that no cat or other enemy should disturb or injure what Maud called "the ornithological depository of their fate."

The direct interest of little Ruth in this affair was not great, for there was no idea of her going to the Bermudas. But she had heard what had been said about this mysterious bird, and although she did not understand it, that did not at all interfere with her curiosity and desire to have an undisturbed look at the little creature which had been choked to death by a message from her Uncle Rodney, who, she thought, should not have spoken so loud if there was any danger of a little bird being at the other end of the wire.

She went up-stairs and entered the room, and as she was a careful little girl, she shut the door behind her. Then she drew a chair up to the table, and, leaning upon it, earnestly regarded the bird. So far as she could see, there was nothing the matter with it except that it was dead; and she knew very well that in various ways and manners a great many birds do become dead. There seemed to her nothing very peculiar in the condition of this one.

Presently, however, she observed something which did seem to her to be peculiar. She drew back from the table, let her hands fall in her lap, and a thoughtful expression came into her face. "Do dead birds wink?" she softly said to herself.

It seemed as if this were really the case, for while she spoke one eye of the bird was, for the second time, slowly opened and quickly shut. While she was pondering upon this strange occurrence a momentary tremor passed through the body of the bird. It was very slight, but her young eyes were sharp.

"It is shivering," she said. "Poor thing! it must be cold!"

She glanced at the window and saw that one of the upper sashes had been lowered. This had been done by her sisters, who had thought the room too warm. She went to the window and found that, even standing on a chair, she could not push up the sash.

Then another idea entered her mind. She went to her own little room, which was on the same floor, and brought back with her her doll's bed and bedstead. She knew perfectly well what a fond mother should do to warm a doll who was too cold. She put the bedstead on the floor, away from the window; then she took off the two little blankets, and, opening the register, laid them upon it. When they were thoroughly warmed she took them to the bed, and, having arranged everything very neatly, she went to the table, tenderly picked up the poor, cold little bird, and carrying it to the bed, snugly tucked it in between the blankets.

Ruth now seated herself upon the floor near by to watch over her little charge, and very soon she saw a decided shaking between the blankets.

"It keeps on being cold," she said. And taking up a little down quilt which was used by her doll only in very cold weather, she placed that over the bird.

This additional covering, however, did not seem to have any effect in quieting the little creature. From shaking, it began to struggle. In a few moments one wing was almost entirely out from under the covering and exposed to the air; and while Ruth was endeavoring to put back this wing the other one came out, and then one leg. When she felt the sharp little claws on her hand she was startled, although they did not hurt her, and involuntarily drew back. In a moment the bird wriggled itself out from between the blankets. Then it hopped into the middle of the bed, and as Ruth put out her hand to catch it, it spread its wings and flew to the back of a chair.

Ruth started to her feet, and as she did so the bird flew from the chair and began circling around and around the room.

THE BIRD BEGAN CIRCLING AROUND THE ROOM.

The little girl did not know what to do. She felt that the bird ought to be caught, or that somebody ought to be called; but before she had decided upon any further action the bird perceived the open window, and, darting through it, was lost to her view.

Tears now came into the eyes of the little girl, and slowly she went down-stairs and told what had happened. Elinor and Maud were shocked and distressed, and even their mother was truly grieved. No matter how things resulted, it would be a great disappointment to the professor not to be able to try his experiments. Ruth was too young to be blamed very much for doing what she thought was an act of kindness, but the girls found great fault with themselves for not having locked the door of the room.

"As it was likely that the bird was merely stunned by the electric current, and frozen stiff as it lay upon the snow," said Elinor, "it might have been easier for the professor to get at the message than if it were really dead. A live nervous system, I should think, would be more likely to retain an electrical impression than a dead one."

"Don't talk that way," cried Maud, "or you will have us all wild to go out and catch that bird. It would be the worst kind of a wild-goose chase, for a bird with a message in him looks just like any other; and even if we had tied a rag to its leg or put a mark on it, I think that by the time it had been chased from field to forest, and had had stones hurled at it and nets thrown over it, its electrical conditions would have been a good deal disturbed. No! We may as well drop this bird of Fate as it has dropped us. I don't believe the message went into him anyway. It simply shot out into the air, and we shall never know what it was until Uncle Rodney reaches England and writes or telegraphs back. Then, of course, it will be too late, and we shall have to be content to wait for the Bermudas until some other winter."

"One thing must be done instantly," said Mrs. Kinton. "We must telegraph to Professor Cupper what has happened. It would be very unkind to let him put himself to any further trouble now that the bird is gone and there is nothing for himself or his friends to experiment upon."

In twenty minutes George was riding to the station with a message which briefly stated that the bird of hope had revived and flown away.

Elinor and Maud went early to bed that night. They had a feeling that this world was a very tiresome place, and there was nothing in it worth sitting up for. But the next morning's mail brought a letter from Professor Cupper which made different beings of them.

The letter had been written late the night before, and was brief and hurried, as the professor wished to get it into the post-office before the last mail closed. In it he said that he had been greatly disappointed and grieved by the news that it was impossible for him to proceed with the most interesting experiment of his life. That was over and done with, but he had been earnestly pondering upon the subject, and had come to the conclusion, for reasons which he would afterward explain, that the message was a favorable one, and that Mr. Carr had told his nieces that they were to go to the Bermudas. The professor had decided to remain in New York for a few days, but would then return and finish his visit; and would give in full his grounds for the conviction that the Christmas present which the girls so earnestly desired had been sent to them.

"I believe it!" cried Elinor. "It is certain that Uncle Rodney sent us a message, and if Professor Cupper, who knows all about these things, says it was the right message, I see no reason to doubt it."

"I don't doubt it," said Maud. "I believe any other kind of a message would have killed that bird as dead as a door nail."

At first Mrs. Kinton felt perplexed, but as she so well understood her brother's generous disposition, and had such confidence in Professor Cupper's scientific ability, she did not feel warranted in opposing the conviction of the professor and the desires of her daughters; and preparations for the trip to the Bermudas were immediately commenced. Of course her brother had sent no money, but it had been arranged how his sister could draw the money on his account.

Fingers now began to fly, and Elinor and Maud felt that the world offered many reasons why they should sit up late. In two days they were in New York, and on the day afterward, with their friends, they sailed for the Bermudas.

Shortly after their departure the professor arrived at Mrs. Kinton's house, and, for the first time in his life, was delighted to find that his young friends were not there. He lost no time in giving Mrs. Kinton his grounds for the opinion he had sent her.

"On some accounts," he said, "it is a pity the bird escaped; but, after all, this matters little, for, alive, it could have been of no use to me. Its emotions on reviving in a state of captivity would probably have obliterated, in its nervous system, all electric impressions. Having, therefore, nothing positive on which to base my judgment, I was obliged to consider the subject with reference to probabilities. The bird was not killed by the electric current; it was merely stunned, and afterward stiffened by lying upon the snow. I therefore infer that the message sent was a very brief one; and, being brief, I infer that it was favorable. Your brother has too kind a heart to say to the girls: 'No;' or, 'You cannot go.' No matter how limited his time, he would have managed to say something in the way of explanation and palliation. On the other hand, 'Yes,' or, 'Go and be happy,' would be all-sufficient. Such a message might merely stun a bird; a longer one might kill it."

"Maud said something of that kind," remarked Mrs. Kinton.

"Maud is a very intelligent girl," said the professor, "and it will not surprise me if she ultimately engages in scientific pursuits. And now, madam," he continued, " how grateful should we be to science! If we had not been able to induce, even inferentially, through the medium of an ordinary bird, the purport of your brother's message, we should have known nothing of his desires and intentions."

"No," said Mrs. Kinton, smiling, "nothing!"

The girls spent a royal two weeks in the Bermudas, and shortly after their return there came a letter from their Uncle Rodney in answer to one in which their mother had given him a full account of the state of affairs. In this letter Mr. Carr wrote:

"As well as I can recollect them, I telephoned to you these words, 'Very sorry, but I can't send the girls this year. Better luck next Christmas! All well?' But I could not wait for an answer to this question, for the whistle sounded, and I was obliged to run for the train. It was much against my will that I sent this message. Affairs had gone badly with me in California; and I found, too, that if I did not very speedily show myself in England I should have heavy losses. I earnestly considered the question on my way toward Afton, but finally decided that under the circumstances I could not afford to give the girls that Bermuda trip. But when I reached England I found my affairs in a great deal better shape than I had any reason to expect. By the time I got down to London, and found your letter, I was already considering what I should do to compensate the girls for the loss of their semi-tropical Christmas; for I knew it was then too late for them to go south with the Sandersons. So when I learned that my message had not been received, and the girls had gone to the Bermudas, I was delighted. In spite of your explanations, I must admit that I do not comprehend how that bird and Professor Cupper managed the matter; but nobody can be happier than I am that they managed it so well."

Maud sprang to her feet, one hand in the air.

"How grateful we should be," she cried, "for the blessings of science!"

A FORTUNATE OPENING.

"WELL, boys," said Mr. Bartlett to a party of his young friends who gathered around him after supper, "I am going to tell you a story, since you are so anxious to hear one, and it will be a story of adventure, but it will have no boy hero. Its heroes are two persons whom you know very well, but I do not think the story will be less interesting on that account."

One of the young people here remarked that he liked stories of adventure about grown people better than those about boys, because boys generally were not allowed to have such good adventures as grown people could have.

"That may or may not be," said Mr. Bartlett. "But to go on with my story:

"When I was about thirty-five years old, and that was a number of years ago, I failed in business and found myself poor. To add to my trouble, my health failed also; and it was considered advisable that I should take a trip to one of the West Indian islands in order to gain strength before beginning business again. My wife went with me, but our little boy was left behind with his grandmother.

"Our affairs were soon arranged. We collected money enough for a trip of a few months, and soon after we set sail for an isle of the sea. This island was a beautiful one, in a charming climate, and here we lived for three happy months; but when at last the time came for us to go, we were perfectly satisfied to do so, and we felt that the object of the trip had been attained.

"We left the island on the steamer *Joseph Barker*, which touched there on a homeward trip from South America, stopping to leave a party of scientific men who had made a special contract to be landed there; and, as the regular steamer would not leave for a week or longer, we were very glad to take passage in the *Barker*.

"We sailed over delightful summer seas for a day and a night and another day and a part of a night, and then something, very mysterious to me, occurred. We ran into a great ship, or rather, the ship, which was under full sail, ran into us. The reason why this seemed mysterious to me was that there were hundreds of miles of unobstructed ocean on each side of us, in any strip of which, forty yards wide, the two vessels could have passed in safety; why, therefore, unless there is some mysterious attraction between vessels at sea, these two should have happened to select the same spot of water for occupation at the same time, I could not imagine.

"The shock of the collision was tremendous; everybody woke up instantly, and many were tumbled out of their berths.

"My wife and I were soon dressed and on deck. There we found a great commotion. The general idea seemed to be that we had sunk the other ship. Immediately after the collision our steamer had backed away, and the two vessels were separated—but where was the other now? It was very dark, but certainly, if she were above water, she would have hung out lights and made signs of distress or desire to relieve distress. But she was not to be seen.

"When our steamer was examined, however, it was found that the bow of the other vessel had struck us on the port side, just aft the foremast, and had made a hole as big as a front door. No one now thought of assisting the other ship. She was, probably, but slightly injured, and it was to her that we must look for help, for it was certain that our ship could not keep afloat long with such a hole as that in its side. Indeed, reports from below stated that she was rapidly filling.

"There were not many passengers, and we gathered together in a knot on the upper deck; some were very much frightened, and all anxious to know what was to be done. A tall gentleman, who was travelling alone, told us what would probably be done. He said rockets would be sent up to indicate our position to the other ship; a gun would be fired; the crew, and perhaps the passengers, would be set to work at the pumps; the donkey-engine would be assigned similar duty, and immediate efforts would be made to stop up the hole. We saw signs, or what we supposed to be signs, of intentions on the part of the crew to do some of these things; but we could not understand what was going on, in the hurry and confusion on the decks.

"The tall gentleman left us to make some suggestions to the captain, who, however, scolded at him in such a way that he came back to us, and was just in the midst of some very ungracious remarks when so unearthly a yell issued from the escape-pipe behind us, that several of us thought the boilers had burst. But the tall man, ceasing his complaints, screamed in our ears that the engineer was merely letting off the steam.

"There is no doubt that the captain and the officers tried to do all that they could, but it was not long before there were evident signs of a panic. It was too dark, even with the lights on deck, for us to see much, but we soon found that there was a general rush for the boats. Then we also rushed.

"The confusion was now so great, and the deafening noise from the steam-pipe made it so impossible to hear any orders, if any were given, while the darkness made everything seem so obscure and uncertain, that I cannot describe how we got into the boats. I know I hurried my wife to a large boat not very far from us, which was just about to be lowered, but it was already so full of people that there was no possible chance for us to get into it. I then ran aft, and found a small empty boat at which two men were working. Without a word, I helped my wife into this, and the two men soon got in, and, one working at the bow and the other at the stern, they let it down to the water. Each man then took an oar and began to pull away from the steamer as fast as possible.

"I suggested that we might take some one else into the boat, but one of the men asked me if I wanted to stay by a sinking craft until it should go down and carry us with it; and then they pulled away even harder than before.

"My wife had said little during all these fearful scenes. She had done exactly as I had told her; our action accordingly had been expeditious, and with as little flurry as was possible under the circumstances. Unrolling a bundle of shawls, which I had thrown into the boat, I now began to make my wife warm and comfortable. This action attracted the attention of the men. We were very close to one another in the boat, and our eyes having become accustomed to the darkness, we could see one another tolerably well.

"'Was that bundle only shawls?' asked the man nearer us. I answered that it was. I had picked up the shawls as we ran out of the stateroom, thinking it might be cool on deck, and had rolled them up and kept them under my arm until we were about to get into the boat. I knew they would be needed.

"The men now stopped rowing for a minute. One of them took up a little water-keg which was in the bow of the boat, and shook it.

"'Nothin' there,' he said. Then some remarks which I did not catch were made about my bundle. I am quite sure that they thought it contained some sort of provision for what might be an extended boat-trip. With their heads together, the two men said a few words, and then sat still as if listening. In a few moments, they began again to row with their utmost strength. Before long they stopped again to listen, and then I heard the sound of oars. They pulled on, and we soon could make out a large boat not far ahead of us.

"'That's not the one!' said one of the sailors, turning around. 'That's the fust mate's boat, an' loaded up. It's the purser's boat we want. That isn't half full.'

"So on they went, stopping every now and then to listen, and it was not long before we heard oars again, at which the men in our boat pulled with renewed vigor. I wondered how they knew in which direction to row, so as to be likely to fall in with the other boats; but I did not ask, for I did not believe the men would stop to answer me. I supposed, however, that boats' crews, on such occasions, might prefer to go with the wind. There was enough wind for us to feel it very plainly. And now we began to near another boat, although it was hard work pulling up to it. I wondered again why they all rowed so hard. They could not be trying to make any particular point. As soon as we were close enough, one of our men hailed the other boat. 'Hullo!' he cried, 'room for anybody else aboard?'

"'How many?' a voice called out.

"I instantly rose in my seat. 'Four,' I shouted.

"'Can't do it,' came back the answer. 'You'd swamp us.'

"Our men made no answer to this, but, bending to their oars, they pulled like madmen. The other boat seemed trying to get away from us, but if this were so it was a useless effort, for we rapidly overhauled it. The moment we came near enough, our bow-oarsman reached out and seized the stern of the other boat. Then both men dropped their oars, and, in a second, they scrambled into the other boat. As they did so, our boat fell behind. I rose to my feet and called out to the other boat to stop, that there were two more in our boat. But no voice answered us, and the boat disappeared in the gloom. For a minute or two I heard the sound of oars, and then even that was lost. We were left alone.

"For a time neither of us could speak. And then my wife began to cry. The cruel desertion by our oarsmen broke down her strong spirit. I tried to comfort her, although I was glad she could not see my face, or know what despair I felt. I told her the men could do us no good, and that we were just as well off without them.

"'You can row,' she said, a little reassured.

"'Oh, yes!' I replied, and I sat down in the place of one of the men, and took the oars, which, fortunately, remained in the rowlocks. I began to row, although I had no idea in what direction I should go. I could not catch the other boats, and it would be of no advantage if I could. The nearest land must surely be several hundred miles away, and besides, for all I knew, I might be rowing toward the Straits of Gibraltar. But the exercise kept me warm, and that was something. I was not thickly clad, and the wind began to feel quite cool. My wife was warmly wrapped up, and that was the only comfort I had. And there we were in the darkness; I gently rowing, and she seated in the stern with her face bent down on her knees, sobbing. Once I heard her say: 'My poor child!'

"The sea was moderately smooth, although there were long, swelling waves, on which we rose and fell. The wind was evidently decreasing.

"After a time my wife raised her head—I had been talking to her, but she had seldom spoken—and she said: 'Do you think there is any chance at all for us?'

"'Oh, yes,' I replied; 'as soon as it is daylight we have a great many chances of being picked up. Perhaps the vessel that ran into us will come back and cruise about in search of us. She probably had to take a long tack before she could return, and she could not expect to come back to the same spot in the dark.'

"She made no answer to this, although I think it must have encouraged her a little, and for a long time we sat in silence; at last she went to sleep. I was very glad to find she was sleeping, for, as she lay upon her side, with her head resting on her arm, I knew that, for a time at least, she would forget her despair and our little boy at home.

"But I felt all the more lonely and desolate, now that she slept. No sound could be heard but the plash of the waves, and nothing could be seen but a little water around the boat. The sky was covered with an even mass of motionless clouds. For some time after we had left the steamer I could hear the sound of the escaping steam. But that was not to be heard now. Perhaps we were too far away, or perhaps she had gone down. And then I thought, with horror, that perhaps she had not yet sunk, and that she might come slowly drifting down upon us, and then, rolling over on our boat, sink us with herself to the dreadful depths below. This idea made me so nervous that I could not help looking behind me, fearing I should see above me the great black hull, with the masts and spars bending down toward us.

"At last I too went to sleep. My head dropped on my breast, and I sat, with the oars still in my hands, and slept, I know not how long. I was awakened by an exclamation from my wife. Starting up, I gazed around. It was daylight; the sky was still cloudy, and, as far as I could see, there stretched an expanse of dull green water, rising and falling in long and gentle swells.

"But my wife was sitting up very straight, gazing past me, with her eyes opened wider than I had ever seen them. She had evidently just awakened.

"'Look there!' she said, pointing over my shoulder.

"I turned quickly, but saw nothing. But then, as we rose upon a swell, I distinctly saw a vessel. It seemed to me to be about half a mile away, but it was probably farther.

"'We're saved!' I shouted, and I took hold of the oars and began to pull with all the vigor that was in me. I wanted to say something, but remember thinking that every word would waste breath and I must row, row, row. It would be death to let that vessel get away from us.

"My wife was as much excited as I was.

"'Shall I wave something?' she cried. I nodded, and she drew out her handkerchief and waved it over her head.

"'If I only had a pole,' she said, 'or something to tie it to!'

"There were two oars behind me, but I could not stop rowing to reach back to get them. She stood up to wave her signal, but I made her sit down again. I felt I must speak then.

"'You must not stand up,' I said; 'you will fall overboard. Is she coming this way?'

"'I think she is,' was the reply. 'She is nearer to us.' And with both hands she continued wildly to wave the handkerchief, while I rowed on.

"Suddenly she stopped waving. For an instant I ceased rowing and looked at her.

"'Go on!' she said, and on I went. Once, when I rowed a little out of the right direction, she told me of my error. She looked straight ahead, neither waving her handkerchief nor saying anything.

"'Are we near?' I said, for my arms were growing lame with the unaccustomed work.

"'Quite near,' she said. 'Row a little more to the left. Yes, I knew it; it is our steamer! I can see the name.'

"I quickly turned. We were within a couple of hundred yards of the vessel. It *was* our steamer. I too could read the words *Joseph Barker* on the stern. She had not sunk yet.

"I don't know how my wife bore up under this terrible disappointment. But she did. She even smiled weakly when she said we might have stayed on board all night, and have taken the boats by daylight—if we had only known.

"The dread of the ship which had haunted me during the night had passed away. I did not care very much whether she sank and carried us down with her, or not. It was a relief to see anything that reminded me of humanity on that desolate, lonely sea. I rowed up quite close to her.

"'Perhaps there is some one left on board,' said my wife, and she and I both shouted as loudly as we could, but no answer came from the ship.

"Then I rowed around her, and we saw the frightful hole in her side. While we were looking at it my wife said:

"'Do you know that I should just as soon be on board that ship as to be in this little boat! I don't believe she will sink a bit sooner than we shall.'

"'I was thinking of that,' I replied. 'The lower edge of the hole in her side is four feet from the water-level when she rolls this way, and nine or ten when she rolls the other way. It must have been because the waves were high last night that the water came in. As long as the sea is quiet, I don't believe she will sink at all.'

"I then rowed up close to the vessel and examined her injuries as well as I could. The side of the vessel, which was a wooden one, did not seem to be damaged below the tremendous gap which the bow of the other vessel had made. The sheathing, as I believe the outside boards of a ship's hull are called, seemed tight enough between the water-line and the hole.

"I agreed with my wife that it would be much better to be on board the steamer than to remain in our little boat, especially as we began to be hungry. Even if a storm should come on, we should feel safer in the larger craft. So I set about trying to get on board. There were some ropes, with blocks and hooks, hanging from the davits from which the boats had been lowered, and, having managed to get hold of one of these, I thought I might climb up it to the deck. But my wife was strongly opposed to this, for, when she saw how the ropes swung as the ship rolled, she declared that I should never go up one of them. And when I came to try the ropes and found that there were four of them together, passing through a pulley above, and that, if I should not pull on them equally, I might come down with a run, I gave up this plan.

"Suddenly I had a happy thought. I rowed to one of the forward davits, and fastened the hook that hung from it to the bow of our boat. I then paddled the boat around until we were under, and very near to, the fractured aperture, which was not far from the forward davits.

"'What are you going to do?' asked my wife. 'We ought not to go so near the ship. She will push us under as she rolls.'

"'I wish to go still nearer,' said I. 'I don't believe there is any danger, with that easy rolling. I wish to get in through that hole. Then I'll make my way on deck.'

"'But what shall *I* do?' asked my wife, anxiously. 'I can never climb in there!'

"'No, indeed!' said I. 'I don't intend to let you try. When I get on deck I'll haul you up.'

"'But can you do it?' she asked, a little doubtfully.

"'Certainly I can,' I answered; and I immediately began to prepare for boarding the ship.

"First, I tied two of the shawls around my wife, just under her arms, making the knots as secure as I could. Then I showed her how to fasten the hook that held the boat into these shawls, when the time came. I insisted that she should be sure to hook it into both shawls, so that if one gave way there might be another to depend upon. I did not like to leave my wife alone in the boat, but there seemed to be no help for it; and, as it could not float away, there was no danger if she was careful.

"When I had given her all the necessary directions I paddled the boat as near to the hole as I could with safety, and then, standing up, I waited until the rolling of the ship brought the lower edge of the aperture within my reach, when I seized it, and in a moment was raised high out of the little boat as the ship rolled back again. I heard my wife scream, but I knew it was only on account of my apparently dangerous rise in the air, and I lost no time in drawing myself up and scrambling into the hole. It was only by the exercise of my utmost strength and activity that I did this. It would have been better if I had made a spring from the boat as soon as I had taken hold, but I did not think of that. Fortunately, the planking on which I was hanging was firm, and I quickly made my way in between the splintered boards and timbers. As soon as I was safely inside, standing on something—I knew not what—I put my head out of the hole and called down to my wife. She was in the boat, all right, a short distance from me, with her face as white as her handkerchief.

"'I was sure you would never get in!' she cried. 'I knew you would drown!'

"'But you see I didn't,' said I. 'It's all right now. I'll hurry on deck, and have you up in no time.'

"For a moment I thought of trying to help her in through the hole, but such an attempt would have been very hazardous, and I did not propose it. She could not have brought the boat up properly, and would probably have fallen overboard in attempting to reach me. So I told her to sit perfectly still until I saw her again, and I withdrew into the interior of the vessel. I found myself in the upper part of the hold, among freight and timber and splinters, and many obstructions of various kinds, but it was not dark. Light came through the hole in the ship's side and also from above. Making my way further into the interior, I saw that the light from above came from the open hatchway in the forward deck. This had probably been opened after the accident, with the idea of lightening the vessel by throwing out part of the cargo. Or it may have been that the men came down that way to investigate the damage done by the collision. It matters not. The hatchway was open, and through it I could probably make my way on deck.

"I was surprised to find no water in the part of the vessel where I entered. I expected to have to wade or swim after I was inside. But the water which had come in was probably far beneath me. The lower part of the hold might be full for all I knew. I had no difficulty in climbing out of the hold. In one of the great upright beams which supported the corner of the hatchway there was a series of pegs, by the aid of which I easily mounted to the deck. There I stopped for a moment, and looked about me. Everything appeared so desolate and lonely that my heart sank. But there was no time for the indulgence of melancholy. I hurried to the upper deck, where the davits were, and looked over.

"'Hurrah!' I cried, 'I'm all right!'

"'I wish I were,' came back the plaintive answer from the figure in the little boat.

"'You shall be, directly,' I said. 'Wait one moment, and I'll haul you up.'

"I now directed my wife to unhook the block from the boat, and to fasten the hook securely in her shawls in the way I had shown her. She immediately rose, stepped from seat to seat, and, unfastening the hook, coolly stood up in the boat to attach it to her shawls.

"I was horror-stricken! 'Sit down!' I cried; 'if you lose your balance you will be overboard in an instant. You can't stand up in a boat, especially when it's rolling about like that.'

"She sat down immediately, but the thought of her dangerous position made me feel sick for a moment. Would she ever be safe on deck beside me?

"She now called up that she was ready, and that the hook was all right. I then took hold of the upper end of the rope which ran through the pulleys in the blocks, and began to haul it in. This soon produced a pressure on the shawls, and my wife declared that if I pulled much harder she would have to stand up.

"'Very well!' I called down, 'you may stand up as soon as you please, now. I have you tight. You may hold on to the block or the hook, if you like, but don't touch the ropes. Now I am going to haul you up.'

"I said this very confidently, but I did not feel confident. I was terribly afraid that I could not do it. I put the rope over my shoulder and began to walk across the deck. As the vessel gave a roll, I felt that I had my wife hanging at the other end of that rope! Now I must do it! If the deck had been stationary, I might have pressed on and slowly pulled her up; but the first time the vessel rolled over toward me I should have fallen backward, had I not grasped the railing which ran across the deck in front of the pilot-house. This railing was my salvation. With the rope over my right shoulder and wrapped around my right hand, I clutched the railing with my left hand, and step by step, and clutch by clutch, I forced myself along. Once I thought of my wife, dangling and swinging above the water; but I banished the idea— my business was to pull, and keep pulling.

"When the vessel rolled toward me so that I was walking up a steep hill, the strain was terrible, but I had advantages when it rolled the other way, and I could throw much of my weight against the rope.

"Now the rope had run out a long way. I was nearly to the other side of the deck. She ought to be up. I glanced back, but there was no sign of her. But I knew she had not fallen off. I could feel her weight. Indeed, it seemed greater than before. Could I, by some accidental attachment, be hauling up the boat? If so, there was no help for it. I must keep on hauling.

"Again I looked back, and, oh, happy sight! I saw the top of my wife's back hair just showing above the side. I gave one powerful pull; I made the line fast to the railing, and then I ran back. There she hung, with her whole head above the side! I ought to have pulled her up higher, but I could not go back to do it now. So I reached over and lifted her in. This effort exhausted what was left of my strength. I managed to take the hook from the shawls, and then we sank down beside each other on the deck.

"THE GULF STREAM GOES TO ENGLAND, DOESN'T IT? DO YOU SUPPOSE IT WILL DRIFT US AS FAR AS THAT?"

"In about half an hour I went below to get my wife some water. I found water in the cooler in the dining-room, and glasses by it. As I filled one of these, I thought of the curious convenience of all this. Here we were, alone on the ocean, and yet I could go down-stairs and get my wife a glass of water as easily as if I were in my own house.

"'Were you frightened when I was drawing you up?' I asked my wife.

"'Frightened!' she answered, 'I almost died! The boat went from under me as soon as the steamer rolled and lifted me up, and then, when she rolled back, I was sure I would be dipped into the water. But I wasn't. And then, when I looked down and saw nothing but that black water moving and yawning there beneath me, and thought of falling into it if any accident should happen, I could not bear to see it, and shut my eyes. I bumped against the vessel every time it rolled, but I didn't mind that. They were gentle bumps.'

"At this moment I happened to think of the little boat. Without attracting my wife's attention, I looked over the side. It had floated away and was entirely out of our reach. I ought to have secured it. But it was of no use to regret the accident now; and, as we began to feel that we ought to have some food, I proposed we should go below to look for some. We easily found the kitchen and a pantry, where there were bread and butter, and a variety of cold meats and vegetables, apparently left from the previous day's dinner. We did not stop to make much of a choice of these eatables, but stood up and ate bread and butter and cold meat until we were satisfied.

"'It is astonishing how hungry we are,' said my wife, 'considering that it is now but very little after our usual breakfast time.'

"But I did not think it astonishing after all we had gone through. The strange thing was that we should have so much to eat. When we had finished our meal and had satisfied our thirst at the water-cooler, we made a tour of the ship—that is, of the more accessible parts of it. We looked into every stateroom. All were empty. We made sure that there was not a soul on board but ourselves.

"When we went into our stateroom we found everything as we left it; and the sight of the berths was so tempting to our tired bodies that we agreed to turn in and take a nap. It was late in the afternoon when we awoke; and when I looked at my watch and jumped to the floor I felt conscience-stricken at having lost so much time in sleep. What vessels might not have sailed near enough to us to have seen a signal of distress, if I had but put one out? And yet, I think that if any vessel had seen the *Joseph Barker* it would have known that something was the matter with her.

"I determined not to run the risk of another collision when night should come on. I found the lamps in the dining-room empty, and supposed that all the lamps on board had probably burned out, and therefore set about looking for oil to fill some of them. I found a can after a deal of searching, and filled a couple of the dining-room lamps. I would have lighted the red and green lights that were burned on deck at night, but they were difficult to get at, and I thought I might not know how to manage them. So I contented myself with hanging a large lantern in the rigging near the bow, and another one at the stern. These were not placed very high, but I thought they would be sufficiently visible. The larger lantern I found in the engine-room, and, to my astonishment, it was burning when I took it down. It seemed the only sign of life on board.

"By the time I had hung out my lights I found that my wife

A FORTUNATE OPENING. 61

had prepared supper, which she had spread on the captain's end of the long table in the dining-saloon. She had no tea or coffee, for there was no fire in the kitchen, but she had arranged everything very nicely, and we really had a pleasant meal, considering the circumstances.

"We did not sit up very long, for the steamer looked extremely lonely by lamplight—and it was so very little lamplight, too.

"The next day, when we went on deck, and looked anxiously over the ocean, not a sign could we see of sail or vessel. We spent a great part of the morning in putting up a signal of distress. This consisted of a sheet from one of the berths, which I fastened to the halyards on the mainmast, and ran up as high as it would go. There was not much wind, but it fluttered out quite well.

"We now began to consider our chances of safety in case we were not soon rescued. I thought, and my wife agreed with me, that if the sea remained smooth the vessel would continue to float; but what would happen if the waves rose, and dashed into the great hole in her side, we scarcely dared to think. We both believed we ought to do something, but what to do we could not determine. The small boat was gone, and our fate was joined to that of the ship. I had heard of fastening a large sail over a leak or break in a vessel, so as to keep out the water to some extent; but a sail big enough to cover that hole would be far too heavy for my wife and me to manage.

"We thought and talked the matter over all day, and the next morning we considered it even more seriously, for the wind had risen considerably. It blew from the south, and, as our vessel lay with her bow to the west—I knew this from the compass on deck—the waves frequently broke against her injured side, and sometimes, when she rolled over that way, the spray did come into the aperture.

"'If we could steer her around,' said my wife, 'so that the other side would be toward the wind, it would be better, wouldn't it? Can't we go into the pilot's house, and turn the wheel, and steer her around?'

"'No,' said I, 'we couldn't do that. You can't steer a vessel unless she is under way—is going, that is.'

"'And is there any way in which we could make her go?' she continued.

"I laughed. The idea of our making this great vessel move was rather ridiculous. But my wife did not laugh. Walking about the ship, we went into the engine-room. We looked at the bright steel cranks and bars, and all the complicated machinery, now motionless and quiet, and down through the grating on which we stood, to the great furnaces far beneath us, where the coals were all dead and cold.

"'This looks as if it were all in order,' she said, 'and yet I suppose you couldn't set it going.'

"I assured her that I certainly could not. I did not know anything about an engine, and even if the fires were burning and the boilers full of steam, I could never hope to turn handles and work levers so that the great wheels would go around and move the vessel.

"'You would probably blow us up,' she remarked, 'and so it is just as well as it is.'

"But later in the day she said, 'Why don't we put up a sail? I have an idea about a sail. If we put one up that ran lengthways with the vessel, like the sail on a sailboat, and the wind kept blowing on this side of us, it would blow the ship over a little sideways, as sailboats are when they are sailing, and that would raise the hole up so that the water wouldn't get in.'

"'It might act that way,' I said. 'But we couldn't put up a sail.'

"'Why not?' she asked.

"'We're not strong enough, for one reason,' said I, 'and don't know how, for another.'

"'Well, let's go and look at them,' said she.

"As it was certainly better to move about and occupy our minds and bodies, instead of sitting still and thinking of all sorts of dangers, we went to look at the sails. There were two masts to the steamer. On the mainmast was a large sail, like a schooner's mainsail, which, I was sure, we could not raise a foot. On the foremast was a square sail, much smaller, and this my wife thought we certainly ought to be able to set. I was not so sure about it. The difficulty in our case would be to get the sail loose from the yard to which it was furled. I had seen the sail set, and knew there was no lower yard, the bottom of the sail being fastened by ropes at the corners to the vessel. I suppose it is easy enough for sailors to go out along the yards and untie—or whatever they call it—the sails, but I could not do it. Nor did my wife wish me to try, when she saw what was necessary.

"'If we had the yard on deck,' she said, 'we could untie the sail and then haul it up again.'

"I knew this would not do, for even if we could have let the yard down, we could never have hoisted it up again, and so, after a good deal of examination and cogitation, I told my wife that we should have to be content to give it up.

"For the rest of that day we said no more about setting sails, but the desire to do the thing had so grown upon me that I got up very early the next morning without waking my wife and went on deck. To my delight I found that the wind had gone down almost entirely. Then, in great fear lest my wife and the wind should rise, I mounted the shrouds carefully, and slowly made my way out on each side of the yard as I had often seen sailors make their way, and with a large knife, which I found on deck, I cut all the ropes which confined the sail, so that it gradually fell down to its full length. I could not unfasten the knots nor comprehend the turnings of the ropes that held the sail, and even to cut them was a work of time and danger to me. But at last it hung down, slowly waving and curling with the motion of the ship; for the swell on the sea still continued. I descended, trembling with the exertion and excitement. By ropes attached to the lower corners of the sail I loosely fastened it to the deck, so that it should be under control in case the wind arose, and then I went aft. I met my wife coming up the companion-way. To her inquiries as to what I had been doing, I told her I had been setting the foresail, at which she went forward to see how I had done it. When she came back she found me lying down on a sofa in the dining-saloon.

I CUT ALL THE ROPES THAT CONFINED THE SAIL.

"'And so you went out on that yard and undid those ropes?' she said.

"I answered that I was obliged to do so, or I could not have set the sail. It is not necessary to report the lecture that ensued, but it was a long and a serious one. When all was over, I promised never to do anything of the kind again, and then we had breakfast.

"From the time when we boarded the steamer we had not

failed, at every convenient moment during the daytime, to look for sails. But we had seen only two, and those were very far off, and had soon disappeared. Our signal of distress was kept flying; but, after a time, we began to wonder whether or not it *was* a signal of distress.

"'Perhaps a white flag on the highest mast means that everything's all right,' remarked my wife.

"I did not know how such a flag would be regarded, but thought that if any vessel could catch sight of our steamer rolling about without any smoke visible, we would need no signal of distress. I wondered that we did not meet other vessels. I had thought there were so many ships on the ocean that, in the course of a day or two, we could not help meeting at least one. But I worked out a theory on the subject.

"'We are probably,' I said to my wife, 'in the Gulf Stream, which flows northward. Vessels going south avoid this stream, and therefore we do not meet them.'

"'But shall we never meet a vessel?' asked my wife. 'The Gulf Stream goes to England, doesn't it? Do you suppose it will drift us as far as that?'

"'Oh,' I said, 'I have no doubt there will be vessels crossing the stream before long. Or one may overtake us.'

"We now had our meals regularly, for my wife had gone to work in the kitchen. She declared it was the most 'cluttered-up' place she ever saw in her life, but she had made wood fires in the curious stove, which it took her a long time to understand, and we had hot tea and coffee and warm food of various kinds. I always sat at table in the captain's place, with my wife, representing the most honored passenger, at my right hand.

"After a brief calm a breeze sprang up, and as soon as we felt it, as we stood on deck, looking out for sails, we ran forward to see what effect it had on our foresail. The great canvas was puffed out and swelling. It made me proud to look at it.

"'Now we shall sail before the wind,' I said, 'if we sail at all. I don't know that one sail will be enough to move the ship.'

"'But how about the waves coming in at the side where it is stove in?' asked my wife.

"'We shall have the wind and waves at the stern of the ship,' I said; 'so that will be all right.'

"She thought this might be so, and we went to the vessel's side and threw over bits of paper, to see if it really moved. Before long it was evident that the steamer did move a little, for the papers gradually began to float backward. When I saw that this was truly the case, I gave a cheer.

"'Hurrah!' I cried, 'she's off! And now let's hurry up and steer!'

"Up to the pilot-house we rushed, and we both took hold of the great wheel. I pulled one side up and my wife pressed the other side down, standing on the spokes with a full appreciation of the importance of her weight. We put the rudder around a little to the starboard, I think it was; and then we watched the clouds, the only points of comparison we had, to see if it steered any. We were pretty sure it did. If the clouds did not move so as to deceive us, our bow had certainly turned a little to the right, and I also found that there was a difference in the swelling of the sail. We then brought the rudder back as before, and the sail filled out again beautifully. Then we knew that we could steer.

"The success pleased us wonderfully. We forgot our dangerous situation, our loneliness, and our helplessness. Indeed, we ceased to consider ourselves helpless. Could we not make this great vessel go, and even alter its course if we chose?

"My wife wished thoroughly to understand the master.

"UP TO THE PILOT-HOUSE WE RUSHED, AND WE BOTH TOOK HOLD OF THE GREAT WHEEL."

"'How fast do you think we are going?' said she.

"I replied that a mile an hour was perhaps as high a rate of speed as we could claim, but she thought we were doing better than that. The Gulf Stream itself would carry us some miles an hour—she had read how many, but had forgotten—and certainly our sail would help a great deal, besides keeping the steamer from drifting along stern foremost.

"'And then,' she said, 'as long as the vessel is moving at all, which way do you think it would be best to steer it?'

"I had been thinking over that matter, and had come to the conclusion that, with our limited facilities for moving the steamer, it would be well to keep before the wind. Indeed, I did not know any other way to sail than this, which was exactly the principle on which, when I was a boy, I used to sail little shingle boats with paper squaresails upon a pond.

"And thus we sailed the vessel. We steered merely enough to keep the wind behind us; and, as it blew from the south, I was well satisfied with our course, for I knew that if we sailed north long enough, we should near some part of the coast of the United States, where we should be certain to meet vessels that would rescue us.

"The wind soon began to grow stronger, and it was not long before we were moving on at a rate which was quite perceptible. We did not remain in the pilot-house all the time. I frequently tied the wheel so that the rudder could not 'wobble,' as my wife expressed it, and went up again when the conduct of the sail seemed to indicate that a little steering was needed. At night I tied up the wheel with the rudder straight behind us—I wish I could express the matter more nautically—lighted our deck-lights, and went to bed. The first night the wind was quite violent, and I was afraid it would blow our sail away, but there was no help for it. I could not take the sail in, nor did I wish to cut it loose, for I might never get it back again if the wind continued. So I saw that everything was as tight and as strong as I could make it, and then I retired in the hope that I would find it all right in the morning, which I did.

"One night—I think it was the fourth night after we set our sail—we were just going below to our stateroom, when my wife looked over the side of the vessel and gave a scream.

"'A light!' she cried; 'a vessel!' I looked and saw it. It was a little speck of light down on the top of the water in the horizon.

"'Look at it!' she said, clutching my arm. 'Now it's down behind the waves—now it's up again! How regularly it rises and falls! Do you think—oh, do you really think it is coming this way?'

"I stood staring at it. At last I spoke. 'It is not a vessel,' I said; 'it is a lighthouse with an intermittent light.'

"She threw her arms around my neck. 'Oh, happiness! happiness!' she cried; 'it is land!' And then she fainted.

"I carried her below and laid her in her berth. I did not try to revive her, but with a chilling sensation of despair I ran to the pilot-house. The thought of land brought no happiness to me. In a few hours we might be beating to pieces on the shore where stood that light of warning. With all my strength I put the rudder around so as to turn the ship's bow away from the light. Whether or not the wind would serve in the new direction I could not tell, but I felt that I must do all that I could—and this was all. I tied up the wheel and went down to my wife. I found her sitting up. To her excited inquiries in regard to our approach to shore, and, as she thought, to a safe end to our strange voyage, I told her that I would avoid, if possible, drawing near to the coast at night—that in the morning we would be able to see what we were about.

"After she had gone to sleep I went on deck again, and I stayed there all night, going below at intervals. An hour or two before dawn the light disappeared altogether. We had floated or sailed away from it—at least I had reason to hope so. When the day broke, bright and clear, I got a glass from the captain's room, but could see no sign of land.

"My wife was much disappointed when she came on deck, but I explained that we did not wish to make a landing in this ship. But if we were near the coast we must soon meet some vessel; so we kept the ship before the wind as well as we could, and waited and looked out, and hoped and feared, and that afternoon we saw a sail.

"It was a small vessel and was approaching us. It grew larger and larger. I made it out to be a schooner. We stood hand in hand, with our eyes steadily fixed upon it. It came nearer and nearer. It was a pilot-boat. Soon we could distinguish a great figure 3 upon its well-filled sail.

"In an hour, apparently, but it may have been in much less time than that, the pilot with four negro men clambered on board. They came up a rope-ladder that I let down to them. I had a nervous time finding the ladder, which I had not noticed until they called for it.

"I cannot attempt to describe our feelings, or the amazement of the men when I told our story. We were off Charleston, South Carolina. I asked the pilot if he could take us in with our sails. He said he thought he could take us along until we could signal a tug, but he did not consent to do this until he and his men had made an examination of our ship's injuries.

"'Can't we go ashore in the pilot's vessel?' my wife asked. 'There are some men on board of it. They could take us in.'

"'No, my dear,' I said. 'Let us stick to our steamer. She has floated well enough so far, and she will bear us to shore, I think.'

"So she consented to stay by the steamer, and she felt better about it when she saw how the men set to work. They went about it as if they knew how. They laughed at our foresail and they set it right. I had not imagined there was anything wrong about it. They hauled up the jib and set it. They raised the big mainsail on the after-deck. The wind was fair and strong, and now the steamer really seemed to move. The pilot-boat sailed rapidly away ahead of us. The pilot thought we had been near the inner edge of the Gulf Stream when the collision occurred. He also thought that our sail had helped us along somewhat during our voyage toward the coast. There had been a strong southeastern breeze during most of the time.

"The next morning a tug met us, and we were towed up to the city, and eventually found ourselves at anchor in the harbor. Our vessel was an object of great interest, and a number of boats came out to us. But we did not go on shore. I refused to leave the vessel or to allow anybody to advise me to do or not to do anything. My wife set to work to pack up our effects.

"I sent a telegram to the owners of the vessel in New York, and a note to a lawyer in the city. The latter came on board in due time, and I put my case before him. By his advice I paid the pilot and the captain of the tug—and this took every dollar I had, with some money I borrowed of the lawyer—and then I made, through him, the formal claim that I had found the steamer abandoned at sea, and that I had brought her into port, having employed and paid for all the assistance I had had, except what was given me by my wife. And I also demanded salvage proportionate to the value of the vessel and cargo.

"This scheme came into my head while the pilot-boat was approaching us at sea. And therefore it was that I declined to go ashore in the pilot-boat, and so abandon the steamer to the pilot and his men.

"There was a lawsuit brought by me. The affair was submitted to arbitration and settled satisfactorily. The pilot made a claim, and, by advice, I allowed him a portion of the salvage.

"The vessel contained a valuable cargo of fine woods, coffee, and other South American products, and, after weeks of valuations, appraisements, and arbitrations, during which my wife went home to her boy, I came into the possession of a sum which was to me a modest fortune. I could again go into business for myself, or I could live upon my income in a quiet way for the rest of my life.

"Very little water was found in the hold of the *Joseph Barker*. The panic among the sailors had doubtless been caused by the sight of the waves through the gap in the side of the vessel, and by the spray dashing through the aperture—the extent of which could not be easily determined from the inside on account of the arrangement of the cargo.

"There was great sorrow and anxiety on the part of the families and friends of the crew and passengers of the steamer, and I received hundreds of letters and many visits of inquiry in regard to the probable fate of those unfortunate persons, but I could tell very little, and that little was by no means comforting.

"In a couple of weeks, however, news came. The ship that had collided with us had not put back; but, at the end of the second day after the disaster, a schooner bound for Martinique had picked up all the boats except our little one and the overloaded boat of the first mate. It had then continued its voyage, no search being made for the steamer, which was supposed to have gone down. The survivors were brought to the United States by another schooner.

"And now, boys," said Mr. Bartlett, "don't you think that was a very fortunate opening for a man in my circumstances?"

"What opening, sir?" asked several of the boys.

"Why, the hole in the side of the ship," said Mr. Bartlett.

"Oh!" exclaimed the boys in chorus.

THE CHRISTMAS TRUANTS.

CHRISTMAS was coming a long time ago, and the boys in a certain far-away school were talking and thinking about it. Eleven of these youngsters, who were all great friends, and generally kept together, whether at work or play, held a secret meeting, at which they resolved that they were tired of the ordinary ways of spending Christmas.

"We are bored to death," said one of the older boys, "with Christmas trees, with Christmas games, with Christmas carols, and with the hanging-up of stockings on Christmas Eve. Such things may do very well for children, but we have grown out of them."

"That's true!" cried the others. "We've grown out of that kind of nonsense."

"Yes, sir!" exclaimed the smallest boy of all, who was generally known as Tomtit. "We've grown out of that."

"Of course," said the biggest boy, who was called by his companions Old Pluck, because he had never been found to be afraid of anything, "there will be this Christmas childishness at the school, just as there has been always; and I propose that instead of staying here and submitting to it, we run away, and have a Christmas to suit ourselves."

"Hurrah!" cried the other boys. "That's what we shall do. Have a Christmas to suit ourselves."

In consequence of this resolution, on the afternoon of the next day but one to Christmas these eleven boys ran away from school, with the intention of finding some place where they would be free to celebrate the great holiday in whatever way they pleased. They walked as fast as they could, little Tomtit keeping up bravely in the rear, although he was obliged to run almost as much as he walked, until they were at a long distance from the school. Night was now coming on, and Old Pluck called a halt.

"Boys," said he, "we will camp at the edge of that forest, and those of you who have brought bows and arrows had better look about and see if you can't shoot some birds and rabbits for our supper. The unarmed members must gather wood to make a camp-fire. But if you are tired, Tomtit, you needn't do anything."

"Tired!" exclaimed the little fellow, standing up very straight and throwing out his chest. "I should like to know why I should be tired. I'll go and bring some logs."

Tomtit was very anxious to be considered just as strong and active as the other boys. Every morning he used to get one of his companions to feel the muscles of his arms, to see if they had not increased in size since the day before.

The camp-fire was burning brightly when the boys with the bows and arrows returned, stating that they had found it rather too late in the day for game, and that it would be better to postpone the shooting of birds and rabbits till the next morning. Old Pluck then asked the members of his little company what provisions they had brought with them, and it was found that no one except Tomtit had thought of bringing anything. He had in his coat pocket a luncheon of bread and meat. It was thereupon ordered that Tomtit's luncheon should be divided into eleven portions, and the little fellow was given a knife with which to cut it up.

It was at this time that there came through the forest a band of robbers—five men and a chief. These men, on their way to their castle, had been talking about the approach of Christmas.

"I am getting very tired," said the chief, "of the wild revelries with which on great occasions we make our castle ring. It would be a most agreeable relief, methinks, if we could celebrate the coming Christmas as ordinary people do. The trouble is, we don't know how."

"You speak well," replied one of his followers. "We would be glad enough to have the ordinary Christmas festivities if we did but know how such things are managed."

The conversation was cut short at this point by the discovery of a camp-fire at the edge of the wood. Instantly every robber crouched close to the ground, and crept silently to the spot where the boys were gathered around Tomtit, watching him as he cut up his luncheon.

In a few moments the chief gave a whistle, and then the robbers rushed out, and each of the men seized two of the larger boys, while the chief stooped down and grasped Tomtit by the collar. Some of the boys kicked and scuffled a great deal; but this was of no use, and they were all marched away to the robbers' castle, little Tomtit feeling very proud that it took a whole man to hold him by the collar.

When they reached the castle the boys were shut up in a large room, where they were soon provided with a plentiful supper. Having finished their meal, they were conducted to the great hall of the castle, where the robber chief sat in his chair of state, a huge fire blazing upon the hearth, while suits of armor, glittering weapons, and trophies of many kinds were hung upon the walls.

The boys were now ordered to tell their story, and when Old Pluck had finished it the chief addressed his captives thus: "I am sure that you young fellows could never have imagined the pleasure you were going to give to me when you determined to run away from school at this happy season. My men and myself have a fancy for a Christmas like that of other people. We want a Christmas tree, Christmas carols and games, and all that sort of festivity. We know nothing about these things ourselves, and were wondering how we could manage to have the kind of Christmas we want. But now that we have you boys with us, it will all be simple and easy enough. You shall celebrate Christmas for us in the manner to which you have always been accustomed. We will provide you with everything that is necessary, and we will have a good old school-and-home Christmas. You shall even hang up your stockings, and I will see to it that Santa Claus for the first time visits this castle. And now, my fine fellows, to bed with you, and to-morrow we will all go to work to prepare for a good old-fashioned Christmas."

The boys were conducted to a large upper room, where they found eleven mattresses spread out upon the floor. They threw themselves upon their beds, but not one of them could close his eyes through thinking of the doleful plight which they were in. They had run away to get rid of the tiresome old Christmas doings, and now they were to go through all those very things just to please a band of robbers. The thought of it was insupportable, and for an hour or two each boy rolled and moaned upon his mattress.

At last Old Pluck spoke. "Boys," he said, "all is now quiet below, and I believe those rascally robbers have gone to bed. Let us wait a little while longer, and then slip down-stairs and run away. We can surely find some door or window which we can open, and I, for one, am not willing to stay here and act the part of a Christmas slave for the pleasure of these bandits."

THEY WERE MARCHED AWAY TO THE ROBBERS' CAVE.

"No," exclaimed Tomtit, sitting up in bed, so as to expand his chest, "we will never consent to that."

The boys eagerly agreed to Old Pluck's plan, and in about half an hour they quietly arose and stole toward the stairs. The full moon was shining in through the windows, so that they could see perfectly well where they were going. They had gone a short distance down the great staircase, when Old Pluck, who led the way, heard a slight noise behind him. Turning to inquire what this was, he was told it was the cracking of Tomtit's knees.

"Pass the word to Tomtit," he said, in a whisper, "that if he can't keep his knees from cracking he must stay where he is."

Poor little Tomtit, who brought up the rear, was dreadfully troubled when he heard this, but he bravely passed the word back that his knees should not crack any more, and the line moved on.

It was difficult now for Tomtit to take a step, for if he bent his knees they were sure to crack. He tried going down-stairs stiff-legged, like a pair of scissors, but this he found almost impossible, so he made up his mind that the only thing he could do was to slide down the broad banister. He was used to this feat, and he performed it with much dexterity. The banister, however, was very smooth and steep, and he went down much faster than he intended, shooting off at the bottom, and landing on the floor on the broad of his back.

The boys were now in the great hall, and seeing a light in the adjoining room they looked into it. There, upon couches made of the skins of wild beasts, they saw the six robbers, fast asleep. A happy thought now came into the mind of Old Pluck. Stepping back, he looked around him, and soon perceived in one corner of the hall a quantity of rich stuffs and other booty, bound up into bundles with heavy cords. Taking out his knife he quickly cut off a number of these cords and gave them to his companions.

"Boys," he then whispered, "I have thought of a splendid plan. Let us bind these robbers hand and foot, and then, instead of doing what they want us to do, we can make them do what we want. That will be ever so much better fun than running away."

"Good!" said the boys. "But suppose they wake up while we are tying them?"

"If we are truly brave," said Old Pluck, "we must just go ahead, and not think of anything like that."

"Yes, sir," said Tomtit, straightening himself and throwing out his chest, "we mustn't think of anything of that sort."

The little fellow was terribly frightened at the idea of going into that room and tying those big, savage men, but if the other fellows did it, he was bound to do it too.

The boys now softly slipped into the room, and as the robbers slept very soundly, it was not long before they were all securely bound hand and foot, Old Pluck going around himself to see that every cord was well drawn and knotted. Then, motioning to the boys to follow him, he went into the great hall, and there he ordered his companions to arm themselves.

This command was obeyed with delight by the boys. Some took swords, some spears, while others bound around their waists great belts containing daggers and knives. Old Pluck laid hold of a huge battleaxe, while Tomtit clapped on his head the chief's hat, ornamented with eagle plumes, and took into his hand a thin, sharp rapier, the blade of which was quite as long as himself.

When all were ready, the boys reëntered the other room, and, with their weapons in their hands, stood over the sleeping robbers. Raising his heavy battleaxe high above the head of the chief, Old Pluck called out to him to awake. Instantly every man opened his eyes, and struggled to rise. But when they found their hands and feet were tied, and saw the boys with their swords and spears standing over them, and heard Old Pluck's loud voice ordering them not to move, every robber lay flat on his back, and remained perfectly still.

"Now, then," said Old Pluck to the chief, "if you do not promise that you and your men will obey me for the next two days, I will split your head with this axe."

"I am willing to parley with you," said the chief, "and will listen to all you have to say; but for mercy's sake put down that battleaxe. It is too heavy for you, and you will let it drop on me without intending it."

"No," said Old Pluck, steadying the great axe as well as he could, "I will hold it over you until we have made our bargain."

"Speak quickly, then," said the chief, his face turning pale as he looked up at the trembling axe.

"All you have to do," said Old Pluck, "is to promise that you and your men will do everything that we tell you to do to-morrow and next day. You will not find our tasks at all difficult, and it will only be for two days, you know."

"Any sort of task, if it lasted a year," said the chief, "would be better than having you staggering over me with that battleaxe. I promise without reserve for myself and men."

"Very good," said Old Pluck, letting down his axe as carefully as he could. "And now we will set you free."

The men were untied, and the boys went to bed, and the next morning all breakfasted together in the great hall. When the meal was over the chief pushed back his chair, and addressed the boys.

"Now, then, my young friends," said he, "what is it that you wish me and my men to do?"

Then stood up Old Pluck and said, "We boys, as I told you before, ran away from school because we are tired of the old humdrum Christmas, and nothing better could have happened to us than to get you fine fellows into our power, as we have done. It will be the jolliest thing in the world for us to see you and your band go through all the wild feats and bold exploits which belong to robber life; and we would like you to begin now, and keep it up all day and to-morrow."

"But what would you have us do?" asked the chief, somewhat surprised.

"I should like to see you sack a village," said Old Pluck. "How would that suit you, boys?"

The boys all declared that they thought that would do very well, to begin with.

The chief turned to his lieutenant and said, "Is there any village round here that has not been recently sacked?"

The lieutenant reflected a moment. "There is Buville," he said. "We haven't been there for six months."

"Very good," said the captain, rising; "we'll sack Buville."

In a short time the robber band, followed by the eleven boys, set out for Buville, a few miles distant. When they came within sight of the village the chief ordered his company to get behind a hedge which ran on one side of the road, and thus stealthily approach the place.

As soon as they were near enough the chief gave a loud whistle, and the whole company rushed wildly into the main street. The robbers flashed their drawn swords in the sunlight and brandished their spears, while the boys jumped and howled like so many apprentice bandits.

"Buville is ours!" cried the chief. "Come forth, ye base villagers, and pay us tribute."

"Come forth!" yelled little Tomtit. "Surrender, and trib!— I mean, pay tribute."

At this the people began to flock into the street; and presently the principal man of the village appeared, carrying a sheet of paper and pen and ink.

"Good-morning, bold sir," he said, addressing the chief. "And what is it you'll have to-day? Shall we begin with flour? How will two barrels do?"

The chief nodded, and the man wrote down on his paper, two barrels of flour.

"Sugar, hams, and eggs, I suppose?" continued the man.

The chief assented, and these were written down.

"Sundry groceries, of course?" said he. "And would you care for any rich stuffs?"

"Well, I don't know that we need any just now," said the chief; "but you might throw in enough gold-threaded blue taffeta to make a jerkin for that little codger back there."

"Three-quarters of a yard of blue taffeta," wrote the man. And then he looked up and asked: "Anything else to-day?"

"I believe not," said the chief. And then, brandishing his sword, he shouted, "Back to your homes, base villagers, and thank your stars that I let ye off so easily."

"Home with ye!" shouted Tomtit, "and keep on star-thanking till we come again."

"You need be in no hurry about sending those things," said the chief to the principal man, as he was about to leave, "except the taffeta. I'd like to have that to-day."

"Very good," said the other; "I'll send it immediately."

As the robbers and boys departed, the latter were not at all slow to say that they were very much disappointed at what they had seen. It was tamer than a game of football.

"The fact is," said the chief, "these villages have been sacked so often that the people are used to it, and they just walk out and pay up without making any row about it. It's the easiest way, both for them and for us; but I admit that it is not very exciting."

"I should say not," said Old Pluck. "What I want is 'the wild rush and dash, the clink and the clank, and the jingly-jank, hi-ho!'"

"That's so!" shouted little Tomtit. "'The clink and the clank, and the jingly-jank, ho-hi!'"

"I think we'll next try a highway robbery," said Old Pluck, "and stop a company of travellers on the road. That must be exciting."

The boys all shouted their assent to this plan, and the robber chief led the way to the nearest highroad.

Here the whole party concealed themselves behind rocks and bushes, and waited patiently for a company of travellers to pass by. It was a long, long time before anybody came, and Tomtit had a sound nap in the shade of a hedge.

At last dust was seen in the distance, and before long five horsemen came riding up. They were all elderly men, and each of them led a mule or a horse, loaded with heavy panniers and packages. With drawn swords and brandished spears the robbers rushed out, followed by the boys, with yells and shouts. Instantly the elderly men stopped and descended from their horses.

"We surrender," said the leader to the robber chief, "but we pray you will not pillage us utterly. We are going to seek a new home for our families, and for the money we get for the sale of these goods we hope to buy the little land we need. If you take these, you leave us nothing."

The chief turned to Old Pluck, and said: "Well, what shall we do about it? Shall we take their goods?"

"If you set out to do a thing," said Old Pluck, "I don't see why you don't do it. There's no sense in backing down."

"That's so!" cried Tomtit, who had just wakened up, and

pushed his way through the hedge. "No backing down. Your money or your lives, travellers. Take notice of that."

"Lead away the horses and mules," said the chief to his men, "and let the travellers go."

As they were leaving the scene of this exploit Old Pluck did not feel altogether easy in his mind. "There used to be a good habit among robbers," he said to the chief, "and that was to give to the poor what they took from the rich. We will go along this road until we meet some really poor people, and we will give them these goods."

The robbers and boys, with the loaded horses and mules, walked along the road for nearly an hour, but met with no poor people. At last the chief declared that it was time to turn and go back to the castle, if they wanted to be there by dinner-time. The boys were very willing to go to dinner, and the whole party retraced their steps.

When they reached the spot where they had robbed the travellers they were surprised to see the five elderly men sitting by the roadside, groaning mournfully.

"What, here yet!" cried the chief. "What's the matter?"

"There is no use going anywhere," sadly replied the leader. "We have no money with which to buy even food to eat, and no goods to sell. We might as well die here as in any other place."

"Boys," exclaimed Old Pluck, after gazing a few moments on the unfortunate group, "I don't believe we will ever find anybody as poor as these travellers now are. Let us give them the goods."

"All right!" shouted the boys. And the loaded horses and mules were delivered to their former owners.

After dinner the boys began to grumble a good deal at the disappointments of the morning.

"We've done nothing yet," cried Old Pluck, "that is half exciting enough, and we are bound to have a good time this afternoon. I go in for burning a town."

"Hurrah!" said the boys. "We'll burn a town!"

"That is a very serious thing," said the chief. "Can't you think of something else?"

Old Pluck looked at him reproachfully. "We want something serious," he said. "What we've had so far is nothing but child's play."

The chief now saw that if he persisted in his objections he would hurt the feelings of the boys, and so he consented to burn a town. A few miles to the south there was a good-sized town, which the chief thought would burn very well, and thither the boys and robbers repaired, carrying blazing torches and firebrands.

When they reached the town and had proclaimed their purpose the inhabitants were filled with consternation. The people crowded into the street, and besought the robbers not to consume by fire their houses, their goods, and perhaps themselves and their children. The chief now took the boys aside, and consulted with them.

"I wish you would consider this matter a little more before you order me to set this town in flames. I am told that there is a magazine filled with gunpowder in the centre of the place, and there will be a terrible explosion when the fire reaches it."

"Hurrah!" cried the boys; "that will be splendid."

"Many of these citizens will lose their lives," said the chief, "and the rest will be utterly ruined."

"Now, look here," cried Old Pluck, "there's no use of always backing down. I'm tired of it."

"Very well," said the chief, "but you yourselves must inform the people of your decision."

"We'll do that," said Old Pluck. "Tomtit, you go tell those

people that the town has got to burn, and there's no use talking any more about it."

"That's so," said Tomtit. "She has got to burn." And with his chest thrown out, and his hands in his pockets, the little fellow boldly advanced to the crowd of people.

As soon as he came near the old men, the women, and the children fell on their knees around him, and with tears and lamentations besought him to intercede with the robbers to save their town. Poor little Tomtit was very much moved by their wild grief and despair. Tears came into his eyes, and his little chest heaved with emotion; but he kept up a brave heart, and stood true to his companions.

"It's no use," he said, "for you to be blubbering and crying. Your houses have all got to be burned up, and the powder-magazine has got to go off with a big bang, and your furniture and beds will all be burned, and the babies' cradles, and—and—I'm awful sorry for it," and here the tears rolled down his cheeks; "but we boys have got to stick by each other, and you won't have any homes, and I expect you will all perish—boo-hoo! But it won't do to back down—boo-hoo-hoo! And the little babies will die; but the old thing has got to burn, you know."

"Now look here, Tomtit," said Old Pluck, who, with the rest of the boys, had drawn near, "don't you be too hard on these people. I say, let the town stand."

The boys agreed with one voice. And Tomtit, kicking one of his little legs above his head, shouted in ecstasy, "Yes, sir, let the town stand, babies and all."

At this the women rushed up to the little fellow, and, seizing him in their arms, nearly kissed him to death.

"I'd like to know what we are to do next," sadly remarked Old Pluck.

"I'll tell you," cried Tomtit. "Let the chief steal a bride."

The whole company stopped and looked at Tomtit. "Little boy," said they, "what do you mean?"

"Why, of course," said Tomtit, "I mean for the chief to seize a fair damsel and carry her off on his horse to be his bride, the wild hoofs clattering amid the crags."

"Hoot!" cried all the boys in derision. And the chief said to Tomtit: "Little boy, I know of no fair damsel to steal, and, besides, I do not want a bride."

"It's pretty hard," said Tomtit, wiping his eyes with his little sleeve. "I've done just what you fellows told me to, and now you won't order anything I want to see."

That night the boys ordered the robbers to hold high revels in the great hall. The flowing bowl was passed, and the great flagons were filled high; wild songs were sung, and the welkin was made to ring, as well as the robbers could do it, with jovial glee. The boys watched the proceedings for some time, but they did not find them very interesting, and soon went to bed.

The next morning Old Pluck called a meeting of his companions. "Boys," he said, "this robber life is a good deal stupider than anything we left behind us. Let's get back to school as fast as we can, and enjoy what is left of the Christmas fun. We will all admit that we are sorry for what we have done, and will promise not to run away again, and Tomtit can go to the master and tell him so."

"I'll be the first one whipped," ruefully remarked Tomtit; "but if you boys say so, of course I'll do it."

The boys now took leave of the robbers, Tomtit having been first presented with the piece of blue taffeta to make him a jerkin. When they reached the school Tomtit told his tale, and he was the only one who was not punished.

The next year these eleven boys were leaving school for a vacation, and on their way home they thought they would stop and see their old friends, the robbers. Much to their surprise, they found everything changed at the castle. It was now a boys' school; the chief was the principal, and each of the other robbers was a teacher.

"You see," said the principal to Old Pluck, "we never knew how stupid and uninteresting a robber's life was until we were forced to lead it against our will. While you were here we learned to like boys very much, and so we concluded to set up this school."

"Do you have Christmas trees, and carols, and games?"

"Oh, yes," answered the principal.

"So do we," said Old Pluck.

"Yes, sir," exclaimed Tomtit, standing up very straight. "No more fire and tribute for us. We've grown out of that kind of nonsense."

THE TRICYCLE OF THE FUTURE.

FRED HUMPHREYS was a boy of an original mind; that is to say, he was very fond of thinking for himself and doing things of which he had never either heard or read. This may or may not be a good disposition in a boy. It depends altogether upon what kind of a boy he is. If he mixes a great deal of reason with his original thinking—if he is able to see when he has made a mistake, and is willing to acknowledge it—and if he is of a prudent turn of mind, and is not likely to dive into a new enterprise until he knows how deep it is and whether or not the current is too strong for him, it may be very well for him to do his own thinking. But if he does not possess these requisites, it would be better, until he is older, to let some one else attend to this matter for him.

Fred was an only son, and his father was desirous that he should find out as much as possible for himself during his boyhood. He was to be a business man, and would probably have a great many ups and downs in the course of his life; and Mr. Humphreys had an idea that if his son could get through with some of the "downs" during his minority, the experience he would thereby gain would prevent his having just as many of them in after life, when they would be much more important.

When the bicycle came into use in this country Fred Humphreys was one of the first boys who had one. When an improved form of the machine was invented Fred sold his old one, and his father added money enough to what he received to buy one of the new kind. This change from good to better occurred several times ; and when the tricycle came before the public Fred gave up his last bicycle, and bought one of the three-wheeled machines, and, after using this for some months, he disposed of it, and became the possessor of a first-class double tricycle, that would carry two persons. Sometimes with his sister, and sometimes with a boy friend, Fred made excursions in this tricycle through the country round about the town in which he lived.

This town was situated in the interior of one of our northern States. It was much frequented in the summer-time as a watering-place, and some of the roads leading to hotels and places of popular resort in the neighborhood were unusually smooth and well made, and, therefore, admirably adapted to bicycles and tricycles. On these fine roads Fred and his machine soon became almost as well known as were the famous "tally-hoes," with four or six horses, which in the season made regular trips between the town and various pleasant spots in the surrounding country.

But, much as Fred enjoyed his tricycle, he became convinced in time that there might be something better ; and as nothing better had, as yet, been invented by any one else, he determined, if possible, to invent it himself. The idea which gradually developed itself in his mind was this : if a boy can pull a vehicle, say, a tricycle, at the rate of a certain number of miles per hour, and with an amount of exertion which he can keep up for a certain time, and if that boy, by getting into that tricycle, and working it with his legs, can propel it at a far greater rate of speed and can keep up the exercise for a much longer time than when he was pulling it —then it must follow that if a horse which pulls a vehicle of any kind could get inside that vehicle and work it with his legs, he could propel it at a much higher rate of speed than when he was dragging it along the ground. And if one horse, why not two, or four? Why should there not be a great tally-ho coach, with six horses working treadmills on the lower story, while crowds of passengers sat above enjoying the rapid and exhilarating excursion? This last idea came into Fred's mind as a picture of the Great Tricycle of the Future. How proud and happy he would be to build and own a machine of this kind! He would sit in front with his hand upon the steering gear, while six fine horses steadily trod the propelling arrangement behind him, eating as they worked, from mangers under their noses; while the ladies and gentlemen who used to crowd the old "tally-hoes" would sit comfortably on the second story, and never tire of telling one another how much better this was than the comparatively slow trips they used to take in the ordinary coaches and carriages.

After thinking over this matter for about a week, and making a good many plans and drawings, Fred determined to try to carry out his invention. He would not set out to build at first a machine for six horses and two or three coach-loads of passengers; but he would attempt to make something much more modest, although constructed upon the great principle that it would be better for the horse to be inside the vehicle and propel both it and himself than to stay outside and pull it. If the comparatively simple contrivance which he proposed to make should work satisfactorily, then it would be easy enough to get sufficient capital to build the grand machine (with driving-wheels twenty feet high and a six-horse team to work it) which, in his mind, he called the Tricycle of the Future.

When he laid his plans and his schemes before his father, Mr. Humphreys considered them very carefully. He had not much faith in Fred's grand idea of the two-storied tricycle with six horses, but he thought that something on a smaller scale might succeed. He agreed with his son that experiments with dogs or goats, which Fred had first thought of, would be a loss of time and labor, because it would be so much trouble to teach these animals to act properly; whereas, an ordinary horse was already trained sufficiently for the purpose. Besides, a dog or goat machine, in Fred's eyes, appeared like a mere plaything, and would not attract the attention of capitalists; but one worked by horses, however rough it might be, would show at once what could actually be done.

Having received his father's consent and the promise of a moderate amount of money for his expenses—for Mr. Humphreys was a rich man, and very generous toward his son—Fred went to work upon the machine, which was intended to show the principle of his invention. It would be a rough affair, but if it worked properly its crudity would not matter; all he wished was to show that the thing could be done. For the building of his machine Fred employed a man who was both a carpenter and a blacksmith; and as he himself was very handy with tools, and this was summer holiday time, he worked nearly all day and was of great help in finishing the thing.

When all was done the new vehicle was indeed a curious affair, and attracted a great deal of attention, especially from Fred's boy friends. It consisted of a strong framework, or floor, at the back of which was a pair of enormous wheels, which had been made for a truck used for hauling great stones and slabs of marble. These were the driving-wheels, and in front was a small but strong wheel, which was turned by a tiller, like the helm of a ship; and with this the vehicle was steered. Between the driving-wheels was set up a machine known in some parts of the country as a "double horse-power," and which is used by many farmers to give motive power to various kinds of agricultural machines. It consists, in the first place, of an inclined floor of slats which moves like an endless chain; and when a horse walks on this the animal remains where he is, but the floor moves, and continually passing from under him and going down to the lower part of the machine, comes up again in front of him. This motion of the floor turns various cog-wheels under it, and a very rapid motion is communicated from them to the machine which is to be worked. The horses are penned in by a low fence, and all they have to do is to walk or tread steadily on, along the moving floor. Some of these "horse-powers" are for one horse and some for two; and Fred had hired a double one from a farmer who lived not far away. This machine was connected with the driving-wheels of his tricycle, and, when horses were put into it and started, the great wheels would be turned, the vehicle would move forward, and the tricyclism of the future would begin.

There were no accommodations for passengers; all that could come afterward. What Fred wanted to show was that a tricycle could be run by horse-power as well as by man or boy-power, the horses being carried along just as the man or boy is carried. In front was a seat for the steersman, who was to be Fred himself, and in the extreme rear was a small platform for his assistant, whose duty it would be to attend to the brakes and to stop the horse-power, when necessary, so that the floor on which the horses stood should become immovable.

A great many opinions were expressed in regard to this new vehicle. Men generally laughed at it; some of the boys thought it would work, while others thought it would not. Among the latter was one, small for his age but old for his years, who was generally known as "Putty" Morris—this name having been given to him by his companions on account of his having a complexion the color of which was not unlike that of ordinary putty.

This youth did not believe in the new tricycle at all. Everything was too heavy and lumbering, he said, and if Fred ever did succeed in setting it going, it would be a very difficult machine to control, and there was certain to be some sort of a smash-up.

"Now, look here, Putty," said Fred, taking him to one side and speaking to him in a manner which he intended should be of service to the youngster, "I've been thinking of asking you to be my assistant; but I wish you to know that I am not going to do it now."

"All right!" said Putty.

"I don't want any boy with me who is a pessimist," continued Fred.

"What's that?" asked Putty.

"Why, that's a fellow who's always thinking that everything is certain to go wrong. Now, I like optimists, who believe that things are sure to go right; that is, as long as there's any chance for 'em. Everybody who ever did anything great in this world was an optimist; for, of course, he wouldn't keep hammering at or fighting out anything if he didn't think it would succeed. Don't you see that?"

"Of course," said Putty, "if a fellow really thought a thing would work, and wanted it to work, he'd better be an optimist; but if he thought the other way about it, why, I think the more he pessimed the better."

"Well, Putty," said Fred, laughing, "if you should twist my machinery as badly as you twist the English language, you'd spoil everything for me very soon. So we'll do without you."

A boy who believed in the new machine, and who was willing to act in the position of brakeman and general assistant, was found in the person of Johnny Hammond, a stout fellow of sixteen, who was always ready for anything of a novel or lively character.

Nothing now remained but to secure the working power, that

is to say, the horses. Fred had hoped that his father would let him have the carriage-horses, but to this Mr. Humphreys objected; he did not wish them used for that sort of work. He had, however, a steady brown mare named Jenny, who was often employed in farm-work, and was accustomed to a "horse-power," and he told Fred that he was welcome to use this animal for his experiment. After some trouble, for horses were much needed by their owners at that time of the year, Fred hired from a farmer an elderly animal known as Glaucus, which had once been, according to tradition, a very fine and spirited horse, but had now settled down into the soberness and placidity of age. Glaucus was tall and bony and not anxious to work, but he had weight and strength, and these are important points in a beast which is to work a horse-power. These two horses did not make quite so good a team as Fred had hoped to have, but, as he said, they did very well to begin with.

It was determined that the trial trip should take place early in the forenoon, before there were many carriages and vehicles on the road, and they did not make any general announcement of the matter, as both Fred and his father thought it would be better to have as few spectators as possible at this first experiment of the running of the machine. If it succeeded, then every one who chose could see it work.

In spite of their precautions, however, quite a crowd of boys assembled to see the horse-tricycle start, and Mr. Humphreys and the man who made the machine were also there. Heavy planks with cross-slats nailed on them were laid from the back of the vehicle to the ground, and up these the horses were led, and placed in the two divisions of the horse-power. The bars were put up behind them, and each horse was tied by its halter to the front rails. The gate of the yard in which the machine had been built

FRED'S IDEAL TRICYCLE OF THE FUTURE.

was opened; Fred climbed up in front and took the tiller, Johnny Hammond mounted the rear platform, and all was ready.

"Take off the brakes, and start the horses!" cried Fred.

Whereupon, Johnny released the big wheels from the pressure of the brakes, and then moved the lever which gave play to the machinery of the horse-power, at the same time starting the horses into a walk. Around went the moving floor on which the horses stood; around and around went the two driving-wheels, and the tricycle was off!

At first it moved very slowly, as was to have been expected, for the ground in the yard was rough; but when Fred had safely steered through the gate, and the tricycle was on the hard, smooth road, it began to go along much more easily. Mr. Humphreys and the man walked by the side of it, greatly pleased with the success of the experiment, while the boys surrounded it on all sides, some cheering and some chaffing; for, although it moved along very well, it certainly was an odd affair to look at. They were in the suburbs of the town, but a great many people stopped to gaze at the horse tricycle, and very soon Fred determined to let every one see that his new vehicle could go at a much faster speed than a walk. The machine was a heavy one, and rather awkward and clumsy in its appearance, but the wheels turned easily on their axles, which were well oiled, while the machinery which connected the horse-power with the driving-wheels was simple and worked smoothly. Therefore, although he could make no such speed as he expected to give to the great Tricycle of the Future, Fred felt sure he could go along at a pretty fair rate, and ordered Johnny Hammond to make the horses trot. Johnny therefore touched up Jenny and Glaucus, and, after some unwillingness, they broke into a trot, and the tricycle began to move over the road at a very creditable speed. Mr. Humphreys and the mechanic soon ceased to follow; and although the boys ran after the machine for some distance, they dropped off, one by one. A few of them tried to climb up behind and enjoy a free ride, but this the sturdy Johnny Hammond would not allow.

Fred steered his tricycle into a wide and handsome road which led to a much-frequented hotel standing on the shore of the lake, about four miles from town. The boy was flushed and happy. The experiment was a success, and he was going along as fast as a horse at an ordinary trot. If he could do so much with a home-made affair like this, what could not be accomplished with a vast machine for six horses, which should be as light and strong and as perfect in all its parts as the finest bicycle or tricycle in the world? Johnny Hammond, too, was in high spirits, and he continually shouted to Fred his approbation of the working of his "gay old machine." The only individual on the big tricycle that seemed to be discontented was Glaucus. He had never been in the habit of going so fast on the horse-power, and besides, there was something in the manner of his progression along the road which seemed to disturb his mind. He tossed up his head, the fire of his youth came into his eyes, and from trotting he began to canter. Johnny's shouts did not moderate his pace, and Jenny, feeling that she must do as Glaucus did, also broke into a canter. Fred shouted to put on the brakes and stop the horses; but this Johnny found to be no easy job. The horse-power was going with such force and rapidity, that the regulating apparatus could not work, and the brakes seemed to take but little hold upon the driving-wheels. Then he climbed up by the side of Glaucus, and, seizing him by the halter, tried to moderate his speed; but he found that the horse was thoroughly frightened, and that he could do nothing with him. The spirit of Jenny, too, was now aroused, and she seemed to be trying to get out of this scrape by running as fast as she could. Fred could do nothing to help, for, if he let go of the tiller for a moment, the steering-wheel would turn round, and the great tricycle would be dashed to one side and be upset and wrecked in an instant.

Fred mentally noted the fact that in a properly constructed machine of this sort there would need to be some way of throwing the driving-wheels out of gear, so that there would be no connection between them and the horse-power. In that case the vehicle could be stopped, no matter how fast the horses were going.

Johnny now again put his whole weight on the brakes of the driving-wheels, but he found this was of no use.

The fact that the road began to slope gently before them, so that they were really going down hill, made matters all the worse, and the panic which seemed to possess the two horses now extended to Johnny Hammond, who, shouting to Fred to save himself while he could, promptly jumped off behind.

Fred was pale and frightened, but he did not jump off. He knew that if he did the tricycle would upset, and the horses would probably be killed ; and besides, he knew well that it would be a very dangerous thing to jump off in front of those great driving-wheels. All that he could do was to stay at his post, and hope that the horses would soon tire themselves out.

The two animals were now working the horse-power at a furious rate ; the few people in the road stood in amazement, or ran after the machine as it passed, while carriages and wagons gave the on-coming tricycle, with its rattling and its banging, and its bounding horses, a wide berth.

Fred was now nearing the hotel by the lake. The broad road led directly to the water, but on one side it branched off into a narrower drive which ran along the shore. It was Fred's intention to turn into this road, because his only safety seemed to be to go as far as he could, and so tire out the horses. But he was dashing on so fast that he made a miscalculation; when he reached the turning-point he did not move his tiller quickly enough, and so lost his chance of running upon the lake road. Now, before him, at a very short distance, lay the lake, and on its edge, directly in front of him, was a row of sheds for the accommodation of the horses and carriages of the visitors to the hotel. Fred's first thought was to steer directly into these sheds, and so stop the mad career of his tricycle; but this would result in a general smash-up, and, as he was in front of everything, he would probably be killed. He did not dare to jump off, as he would have to jump directly in front of the driving-wheels. There seemed nothing for him to do but to steer into the lake. If this had to be done, the deeper the water into which he plunged the better; and with this idea in his mind, he deftly guided his machine past the sheds, and toward a pier which extended a short distance into the lake. Thundering upon the plank floor came the great tricycle, and in the next instant it had gone off the end of the pier and down into the water.

There was a huge splash; there were shouts from the hotel and from the road; a fountain of spray shot high into the air, and then a foaming, whirling, gurgling pool closed over the spot where the great dive had been made. Down to the bottom of the lake sank, not only Fred's Tricycle of the Present, but his ideal Tricycle of the Future, with its two stories, its beautifully working machinery, its crowds of passengers, and its wonderful achievements. There was nothing of the kind now for Fred but a wrecked and sunken Tricycle of the Past.

At the moment the steering-wheel left the edge of the pier Fred made a wild spring into the water, and so went down by himself, off at one side of the descending machine. As he sank, thoughts and ideas passed through Fred's mind as rapidly as if they were being telegraphed on a wire. One of these was that all he had been working for so hard had now come to a disastrous end; for his father would never more allow him to have anything to do with such an unmanageable machine as a horse-tricycle. But the thought that overshadowed everything else was the fate of those poor horses! They were tied to the horse-power by their halters, and would, therefore, be kept down at the bottom of the lake, and be drowned. There was so much heavy iron-work about the machinery, it would certainly hold them there like an anchor. Fred had no fears in regard to himself. No thought of sorrow-stricken parents or weeping friends passed through his mind; he had been down to the bottom of the lake before, and although he was encumbered with clothing his coat was thin, his shoes were light, and he knew that he could swim to shore.

In a very short time he rose to the top of the water and began to strike out for the pier. Then, some distance behind him, came up the head of a horse, and Jenny, with a little snort, went swimming landward. Now appeared another horse's head, and Glaucus, with wildly staring eyes, came floundering up, and, after gazing about in much amazement, made for a distant point along the shore, as if he did not wish to land at a place where he had come to such grief. Last of all, up came Putty Morris, his hair dripping with water, and his mouth spluttering vigorously as he slowly swam shoreward.

When Fred reached the pier and had taken one of the dozen hands which were extended to him from the little crowd of people who had hurried there, he was quickly pulled up, and whatever he had intended to say was cut short by his astonishment at seeing Jenny just coming to land. Then, turning around, his amazement was increased by the sight of Glaucus, still making for his distant point. But when he beheld Putty Morris, spluttering and paddling steadily for the pier, Fred's hair, wet as it was, felt as if it would like to stand on end.

"Do you live down there?" he said to Putty, a moment later, when that dripping boy was hauled upon the pier.

"Not exactly," was the answer, after several vigorous shakes and puffs; "and if I'd known that you were going to take me to the bottom of the lake, you may be sure I'd never have jumped aboard your crazy old machine."

"How did you come to do it?" asked Fred. "I didn't know you were there."

"Well," said Putty, "I was up the road there, and saw you coming like a lot of wild Indians. I saw Johnny Hammond jump off, and guessed something was the matter. Before the thing was up to me I knew that the horses were running away, or trying to, and that you were hanging on to your steering gear with a rather pessimy look on your face, and that you couldn't let go to do anything with the horses. So I ran after you, and climbed up behind, and I had to be a pretty lively hoptimist to do it, I can tell you. All I could try to do was to get you rid of your horses, and I thought that if I untied their halters and took down their bars they'd slide out behind, and then you'd stop. I didn't say anything to you, for there was such a noise I didn't suppose you'd hear me; and just as I unfastened the second halter we were out on the pier, and before I had time to jump, down we all went together!"

"Fred," said Putty Morris to his friend a few days after these events, "are you going to make any more of your big machines?"

"Well, no," said Fred, "not at present. These things can't be done without money, and father is rather touchy on that subject just now. He has had to pay for that double horse-power and everything else is a dead loss; and besides that, old Glaucus scraped his leg in the scrimmage, and he'll not be fit to be used for a month. I am going to begin again at the very bottom round, and if I run anything else of the kind this summer, I shall get a unicycle."

"A unicycle!" exclaimed Putty; "what is that?"

"Why, don't you know?" said Fred. "There goes a fellow with one now."

THE ACCOMMODATING CIRCUMSTANCE.

IT was on a bright afternoon, many, many years ago, that a young baron stood on the stone steps that led down from the door of his ancestral home. That great castle was closed and untenanted, and the baron was taking leave of it forever. His father, who was now dead, had been very unfortunate, and had been obliged to sell his castle and his lands. But he had made it a condition that the nobleman who bought the estate should allow the young baron to occupy it until he was twenty-one years of age.

This period had now arrived, and although the purchaser, who did not need the castle, had told the baron that he might remain there as long as he chose, the young man was too high-spirited to depend upon the charity of any one, and he determined to go forth and seek a fortune for himself. His purpose was to go to the town of the Prince of Zisk, a journey of a few days, and to offer to join an army which the prince intended to lead against a formidable band of robbers which had set up a stronghold in his dominions. If he should distinguish himself in this army, the young baron hoped that he might rise to an honorable position. At any rate, he would earn a livelihood for himself, and be dependent upon no one.

But it was a very sad thing for him to leave this home where he was born, and where he had spent most of his life. His parents were dead, he had no relatives, and now he was to leave the house which had been so dear to him. He stood with one foot upon the ground, and the other upon the bottom step, and looked up to the great hall door which he had shut and locked behind him, as if he were unwilling to make the movement which would finally separate him from the old place.

As he stood thus he heard some one approaching, and, turning, he saw an old woman and a young girl coming toward the castle. Each carried a small bundle, and, besides these, the young girl had a little leathern bag, which was fastened securely to her belt.

"Good sir," said the old woman, "can you tell me if we can rest for the night in this castle? My granddaughter and I have walked since early morning, and I am very tired. It is a long time since we have passed a house, and I fear we might not come to another one to-day."

The baron hesitated for a moment. It was true that there was no other house for several miles, and the old woman looked as if she was not able to walk any farther. The castle was shut up and deserted, for he had discharged his few servants that morning, and he was just about to leave it himself; but, for all that, he could not find it in his heart to say that there was no refuge there for these two weary travellers. His family had always been generous and hospitable, and although there was very little that he could offer now, he felt that he must do what he could, and not send away an old woman and a young girl to perish on the road in the cold winter night which was approaching.

"The castle is a bare and empty place," he said, "but you can rest here for the night." And so saying he went up the steps, opened the door, and invited the travellers to enter.

Of course if they stayed there that night, he must do so also, for he could not leave the castle in the care of strangers, although these appeared to be very inoffensive people. And thus he very unexpectedly reëntered the home he thought he had left forever.

There was some wood by the fireplace in the great hall, and the baron made a fire. He had left no provisions in the house, having given everything of the kind to the servants, but he had packed into his wallet a goodly store of bread, meat, and cheese, and with these he spread a meal for the wayfarers. When they had been strengthened by the food and warmed by the fire, the old woman told her story.

"You must not think, kind sir," she said, "that we are poor outcasts and wanderers. I have a very pleasant little home of my own, where my granddaughter and myself have lived very happily ever since she was a little baby, and now, as you see, she is quite grown up. But Litza—that is her name—has a godmother who is a very peculiar person, whom we are all obliged to obey, and she came to us yesterday and gave Litza a little iron box, which is in that leathern bag she carries, and charged her to start with me the next morning, and take it to its destination."

In order to account for the condition of his house, the baron then told his story. Litza and her grandmother were grieved to hear the account of the young nobleman's ill fortune, and the old woman said if they prevented his journey they might yet try to go on.

"Oh, no," said the baron. "I was starting too late anyway, for it had taken me so long to bid good-by to my old home. It will be just as well for me to go to-morrow. So you and your granddaughter shall have a room here to-night, and all will be well."

The next morning, after a breakfast which quite finished the baron's provisions, the three set out together, as their roads lay in the same direction. About noon the old woman became very tired and hungry. There was no house in sight, and the road seemed quite deserted.

"If I had known it would be so far," she said to herself, "we would not have come. I am too old to walk for two days. If I could only remember the meaning of the words, I would surely try them now. But I cannot remember—I cannot remember."

When this old woman was a little girl, she had lived with Litza's godmother, who was the daughter of a magician, and was now over a hundred years old. From this person she had learned five magical words, which, when repeated, would each bring up a different kind of goblin or spirit. In her youth Litza's grandmother had never used these words, for she was a timid girl; and now for years, although she remembered the words, she had entirely forgotten what sort of creature each one would call forth. Some of these beings were good, and some she knew were very bad, and so, for fear of repeating the wrong word, she had never used any one of them. But now she felt that if ever she needed the help of goblin or fairy, she needed it this day.

"I can walk no farther," she said, "and that young man cannot carry me. If I do not use my words, I must perish here. I will try one of them, come what may." And so, with fear and trembling, she repeated aloud the third word.

Instantly there appeared before her a strange being. He was of a pale pea-green color, with great black eyes, and long arms and legs which seemed continually in motion. He jumped into the air, he snapped his fingers over his head, and suddenly taking from his pockets two empty bottles and an earthen jar, he began tossing them in the air, catching them dexterously as they fell.

"Who on earth are you?" said the old woman, much astonished.

"I am the Green Goblin of the Third Word," replied the other, still tossing up his jar and bottles; "but I am generally known as the Accommodating Circumstance."

"I don't know exactly what that may be," said the old woman, "but I wish that instead of a juggler with empty bottles and jars, you were a pastry-cook with a basket full of something to eat."

Instantly the goblin changed into a pastry-cook carrying a large basket filled with hot meat pies and buns. The old woman jumped to her feet with delight, and beckoned to the others, who had just turned round to see where she was.

"Come here," she cried. "Here is a pastry-cook who has arrived just in the nick of time."

The party now made a good meal, for which the old woman would not allow the baron to pay anything, as it was a repast to which she had invited him. And then they moved on again, the pastry-cook following. But although the grandmother was refreshed by the food, she was still very tired. She fell back a little and walked by the side of the pastry-cook.

"I wish," she said, "that you were a man with a chair on your back. Then you might carry me."

Instantly the pastry-cook changed into a stout man in a blue blouse, with a wooden armchair strapped to his back. He stooped down, and the old woman got into the chair. He then walked on, and soon overtook the baron and Litza.

"Ah!" cried the old woman, "see what good fortune has befallen me! The pastry-cook has gone, and this man with his chair has just arrived. Now I can travel with ease and comfort."

"What wonderful good fortune!" cried Litza.

"Wonderful good fortune, indeed!" exclaimed the baron, equally pleased.

The four now pursued their way, the old woman comfortably

nodding in the chair, to which the baron had secured her with his belt. In about an hour the road branched, and the baron asked the chairman which way led to the town of Zisk. But the man, who was a dull, heavy fellow, did not know, and the baron took the road to the right. After walking two or three miles they came to a wide river, at the edge of which the road stopped. On a post was a signboard on which was painted, "Blow ye horn for ye ferryman." Below this hung a large horn, with a small pair of bellows attached to the mouthpiece.

"That is a good idea,' said the baron. "One ought to be able to blow a horn very well with a pair of bellows." And so saying, he seized the handle of the bellows and blew a blast upon the horn that made Litza and her grandmother clap their hands to their ears. "I think that will bring the ferryman," said the baron, as he helped the old woman to get out of her chair.

In a few minutes they heard the sound of oars, and a boat made its appearance from behind a point of land to the right. To their surprise it was rowed by a boy about fourteen years old. When the boat touched the shore they all got in.

"I am afraid you cannot row so heavy a load," said the baron to the boy; "but perhaps this good man will help you."

The boy, who was well dressed and of a grave demeanor, looked sternly at the baron. "Order must be kept in the boat," he said. "Sit down, all of you, and I will attend to the rowing." And he began to pull slowly but steadily from the shore. But instead of rowing directly across the river, he rounded the high point to the right, and then headed toward an island in the stream.

"Where are you taking us?" asked the baron.

"This is the place to land," replied the boy, gruffly. And in a few strokes he ran the boat ashore at the island.

A large house stood not far away from the water, and the baron thought he would go there and make some inquiries, for he did not like the manner of the boy in the boat. He accordingly stepped ashore, and, followed by the rest of his party, approached the house. When they reached it they saw over the door, in large black letters, the words, "School for Men." Two boys, well dressed and sedate, came out to meet them, and ushered them in.

"What is this place?" asked the baron, looking about him.

"It is a school," was the reply, "established by boys for the proper instruction and education of men. We have found that there are no human beings who need to be taught so much as men; and it is to supply this long-felt want that we have set up our school. By diverting the ferry from its original course we have obtained a good many scholars who would not otherwise have entered."

"What do you teach men?" asked the baron.

"The principal thing we try to teach them," said the other, "is the proper treatment of boys. But you will know all about this in good time."

"What I wish most now to know," said the baron, smiling, "is whether or not we can all obtain lodging here to-night. It is already growing dark."

"Did these two ladies come with you?" asked the boy.

"Yes," answered the baron.

"It was very good of them," said the boy. "Of course they can stay here all night. We always try to accommodate friends who come with scholars."

It was past supper time at the school, but the baron and his party were provided with a good meal, and Litza and her grandmother were shown to a guest chamber on the ground floor. One boy then took charge of the chair-carrier, while another conducted the baron to a small chamber up-stairs, where he found everything very comfortable and convenient.

"You can sit up and read for an hour or two," said the boy. "We don't put our scholars all into one great room like a barrack, and make them put out their lights and go to bed just at the time when other people begin to enjoy the evening."

When the baron arose the next morning he was informed that the principal wished to see him, and he was taken down-stairs into a room where there was a very solemn-looking boy sitting in an armchair before a fire. This was the principal, and he arose and gravely shook hands with the baron.

"I am glad to welcome you to our school," he said, "and I hope you will do honor to it."

"I have no intention of remaining here," said the baron.

The principal regarded him with a look of great severity. "Silence, sir!" he said. "It pains me to think of the sorrow which would fill the hearts of your children or your young relatives if they could hear you deliberately declare that you did not wish to avail yourself of the extraordinary educational opportunities which are offered to you here."

The principal then rang a bell, and two of the largest scholars, who acted as monitors, entered the room. "Take this new pupil," he said to them, "to the schoolrooms, and have him entered in the lowest class. He has much to learn."

The baron saw that it would be useless to resist these two tall fellows, who conducted him from the room, and he peacefully followed them to the large schoolroom, where he was put in a class and given a lesson to learn.

The subject of the lesson was the folly of supposing that boys ought not to be trusted with horses, battleaxes, and all the arms used in war and hunting. There were twelve reasons proving that men were very wrong in denying these privileges to boys, and the baron was obliged to learn them all by heart.

At the other end of the room he saw the chair carrier, who was hard at work over a lesson on the wickedness of whipping boys. On the wall, at one end of the room, was the legend in large letters, "The Boy: Know Him, and You are Educated." At the other end were the words, "Respect your Youngers."

In the afternoon the baron studied sixteen rules which proved that boys ought to be consulted in regard to the schools they were sent to, the number of their holidays, the style of their new clothes, and many other things which concerned them more than any one else. At the end of the afternoon session the principal made a short address to the school, in which he said that in four days it would be Christmas, at which time the scholars would have a month's holiday.

"We believe," he said, "that scholars ought to have at least that much time at Christmas; and, besides, your instructors need relaxation. But," said he, with a severe look at the baron, "disaffected new-comers must not suppose that they will be allowed this privilege. Such pupils will remain here during the holidays."

After this speech school was dismissed, and the scholars were allowed three hours to play.

The baron was disturbed when he found that he would not be permitted to leave. He had heard that the Prince of Zisk intended to start on his expedition immediately after Christmas; and if he did not get to the town very soon he could not join his army. So he determined to escape.

Walking about, he met Litza and her grandmother. The old woman was much troubled. She had been told that she could leave whenever she chose, but she felt she could not go away without the chair-carrier, and he was detained as a pupil. She would not explain her trouble to her granddaughter, for she did not wish her to know anything about the magical nature of the assistance she had received. In a few moments the chair-carrier also made his appearance, and then the baron, seeing that none of the boys were in sight, proposed that they should go down to the beach and escape in a ferry-boat.

The boat was found there, with the oars, and they all jumped in. The baron and the chair-carrier then each seized an oar and pushed off. They were not a dozen yards from the shore when several of the boys, accompanied by some of the larger pupils, came running down to the beach. The baron could not help smiling when he saw them, and, resting on his oar, he made a little speech.

"My young friends," he said, "you seem to have forgotten, when you set up your school, that men, when they become scholars, are as likely to play truant as if they were boys."

To these remarks the boy teachers made no answer, but the big scholars on shore looked at each other and grinned. Then they all stooped down and took hold of a long chain that lay coiled in the shallow water. They began to pull, and the baron soon perceived that the other end of the chain was attached to the boat. He and the chair-man pulled as hard as they could at the oars, but in spite of their efforts they were steadily drawn to shore. Litza and her grandmother were then sent to their room, while the baron and the chair-man were put to bed without their suppers.

The next day the old grandmother walked about by herself, more troubled than ever, for she was very anxious that Litza should fulfil her mission, and that they should get back home before Christmas. And yet she would not go away and leave her magical companion. Just then she saw the chair-carrier looking out of a second-story window, with a blanket wrapped around him.

"Come down here," she said.

"I can't," he answered. "They say I am to stay in bed all day, and they have taken away my clothes."

"You might as well be back with your goblin companions," said the old woman, "for all the use you are to me. I wish you were somebody who could set things straight here."

Instantly there stood by her side a school trustee. He was a boy of grave and pompous demeanor, handsomely dressed, and carrying a large gold-headed cane.

"My good woman," he said, in a stately voice, "is there anything I can do to serve you?"

"Yes, sir," she replied. "My granddaughter and I," pointing to Litza, who just then came up, "wish to leave this place as soon as possible, and to pursue our journey."

"Of course you may do so," said he. "This is not a school for women."

"But, grandma," said Litza, "it would be a shame to go away without the poor baron, who is as anxious to get on as we are."

"There is a gentleman here, sir," said the old woman, "who does not wish to stay."

"Did you bring him?" asked the trustee.

"Yes, sir; he came with us."

"And you wish to take him away again?" said he.

"Yes, sir; we do," said Litza.

"Very well, then," said the trustee, severely, "he shall be dismissed. We will have no pupils here whose children or guardians desire their removal. I will give orders in regard to the matter."

In a few moments the baron's clothes were brought to him, and he was told that he might get out of bed and leave the establishment. When he came down and joined Litza and her grandmother, he looked about him and said: "Where is the chair-carrier? I cannot consent to go away and leave him here."

"Do not trouble yourself about that man," said the grandmother; "he has already taken himself away."

The party, accompanied by the trustee, proceeded to the boat, where the boy ferryman was waiting for them. To the surprise of the baron the trustee got in with them, and they were all rowed to the other side of the river, where they found the road that led to Zisk. The school trustee walked with them, delivering his opinions in regard to the education of men. The baron grew very tired of hearing this talk.

"I am much obliged to this person," he thought, "for having enabled me to get away from that queer school; but he certainly is a dreadful bore. I wish he were going on some other road."

Litza and her grandmother agreed with the baron, and the old woman would gladly have changed the trustee into a chair-carrier again, but she had no opportunity of doing so, for the pompous little fellow never fell back behind the rest of the party, where he could be transformed unobserved. So they all walked on together until they reached the middle of a great plain, when suddenly a large body of horsemen appeared from behind a clump of trees at no great distance.

"It is a band of robbers!" said the baron, stopping, and drawing his sword. "I know their flag. And they are coming directly toward us."

The grandmother and Litza were terribly frightened, and the baron turned very pale, for what could his one sword do against all those savage horsemen? As for the school trustee, he was glad to fall back now, and he crouched behind the baron, nearly scared out of his wits. He even pushed the old woman aside, so as to better conceal himself.

"You wretched coward!" she exclaimed. "I wish you were somebody able to defend us against these robbers."

Instantly there was a great clank of steel, and in the place of the trustee there stood an immense man, fully eight feet high, clothed in mail, and armed to the teeth. At his left side he carried a great sword, and on the other a heavy mace. In his hand he held a strong bow, higher than himself, his belt was filled with daggers and arrows, and at his back was an immense shield.

"Hold this in front of your party," he said to the baron, setting the shield down before him, "and I will attend to these rascals."

Quickly fitting a long arrow to his bow, he sent it directly through the foremost horseman, and killed a man behind him. Arrow after arrow flew through the air, until half the robbers lay dead on the field. The rest turned to fly, but the armed giant sprang in among them, his sword in one hand and his mace in the other, and in less than five minutes he had slain every one of them.

"Now, then," said he, returning, and taking up his bow and shield, "I think we may proceed without further fear."

The baron and Litza were no less delighted at their deliverance than surprised at the appearance of this defender, and the old woman was obliged to explain the whole matter to them. "I did not want you to know anything about it," she said to Litza, "for a young girl's head should not be filled with notions of magic; but the case was very urgent, and I could not hesitate."

"I am very glad you did not hesitate," said the baron, "for in a few minutes we should all have been killed. There was certainly never anything so useful as your Accommodating Circumstance."

The armed giant was a quiet and obliging fellow, and he offered to carry the old woman on his shoulder, which she found a very comfortable seat.

Toward evening they arrived in sight of the town of Zisk, and the baron said to the grandmother, "I am very much afraid you will lose your giant, for when the prince sees such a splendid soldier he will certainly enlist him into his army."

"Oh, dear!" cried the old woman, slipping down from the giant's shoulder. "I wish this great fellow was somebody who could not possibly be of any use to the prince as a soldier."

Instantly there toddled toward her a little baby about a year old. She had a white cap on her funny little head, and was very round and plump. She had scarcely taken three steps when she stumbled and sat down very suddenly, and then she began to try to pull off one of her little shoes. They all burst out laughing at this queer little creature, and Litza rushed toward the baby and snatched her up in her arms.

"You dear little thing!" she said. "the prince will never take you for a soldier."

"No," said the baron, laughing. "and she can never grow up into one."

It was too late for the baron to see the Prince of Zisk that day, and the party stopped for the night at a little inn in the town. The next morning, as the baron was about to go to the palace, he asked Litza what was her business in Zisk, and if he could help her.

"All my godmother told me to do," said the young girl, "was to give this box to the noblest man in Zisk, and of course he is the prince."

"Yes," said the baron; "and as I am on my way to the palace, I may help you to see him."

"Go you with the baron," said the grandmother to Litza. "and I will stay here and take care of this baby. And as soon as you come back I will change her into a long-legged man with two chairs on his back, and we will get home to my cottage as fast as we can."

When the baron and the young girl reached the palace they found the prince in his audience-chamber, surrounded by officers and courtiers. Litza stood by the door, while the baron approached the prince and respectfully told him why he had come.

"You are the very man we want!" cried the prince. "I have conceived a most admirable plan of conquering my robber foes, and you shall carry it out. The day after to-morrow is Christmas, and these highwaymen always keep this festival as if they were decent people and good Christians. They gather together all their wives and children, and their old parents, and they sing carols and make merry all day long. At this time they never think of attacking anybody or of being attacked, and if we fall upon them then we can easily destroy them all, young and old, and thus be rid of the wretches forever. I have a strong body of soldiers ready to send, but they must be led by a man of rank, and all my officers of high degree wish to remain here with their families to celebrate Christmas. Now you are a stranger, and have nothing to keep you here, and you are the very man to lead my soldiers. Destroy that colony of robbers, and you shall have a good share of the booty that you find there."

"Oh, prince!" exclaimed the baron, "would you have me, on holy Christmas Day, when these families are assembled together to celebrate the blessed festival, rush upon them with an armed band, and slay them, old and young, women and children, at the very foot of the Christmas tree? No man needs occupation more than I, but this is a thing I cannot do."

"Impudent upstart!" cried the prince, in a rage; "if you cannot do this, there is nothing for you here. Begone!"

Without an answer the baron turned and left the hall. Litza, who still stood by the door, did not now approach the prince, but ran after the baron, who was walking rapidly away. "This is yours," she said, taking the iron box from her little bag. "You are the noblest man."

The baron, surprised, objected to receiving the box, but Litza was firm. "I was told," she said, "to give it to the noblest man in Zisk, and I have done so."

When the baron found that he must keep the box he asked Litza what was in it.

"I do not know," said Litza; "but the key is fastened to the handle."

They sat down under a tree, in a quiet corner of the palace grounds, and opened the box. Something inside was covered with a piece of velvet, on top of which lay a golden locket. The baron opened it, and beheld a portrait of the beautiful Litza.

"Why, you have given me yourself!" he cried, delighted.

"So it appears," said Litza, looking down upon the ground.

"And will you marry me?" he cried.

"If you wish it," said Litza. So that matter was settled.

The two then went to the inn, and told the grandmother what had occurred. She looked quite pleased when she heard this story, and then she asked what else was in the box.

"I found so much," said the baron, "that I did not think of looking for anything more." He then opened the box, and, lifting the piece of velvet, found it filled with sparkling diamonds.

"That is Litza's dowry," cried the old woman. "It was a wise thing in her godmother to send her out to look for a noble husband, for one would never have come to my little cottage to look for her. But it seems to me that the box might as well have been given to you at your castle. It would have saved us a weary journey."

"But if we had not taken that journey," said Litza, "we should not have become so well acquainted, and I would not have known he was the noblest man."

"It is all right," said the grandmother, "and your dowry will enable the baron to buy his castle again, and to live there as his ancestors did before him."

The grandmother desired to leave Zisk immediately, but the baron objected. "There is something I wish to do to-day," he said; "and if we start early to-morrow morning on horseback we can reach my castle before dark."

The old woman agreed to this, and the baron continued: "I would like you to lend me the baby for the rest of the day; and when the sun-dial in the courtyard shall mark three hours after noon you will please open this piece of paper and wish what I have written upon it."

The grandmother took the folded piece of paper, and let him have the baby. She and Litza wondered much what he was going to do, but they asked no questions.

The baron had learned that it was a three hours' walk from the town to the stronghold of the robbers, and just at noon he set out for that place, carrying the baby in his arms. Before he had gone a mile he wished that the baby had been changed into somebody who could walk, but it was too late now.

At three hours after noon the grandmother was about to open the paper, when Litza exclaimed, "Before you wish anything, dear grandmother, let me read what the baron has written."

Litza then took the paper and read it. "It is just what I expected," she cried. "He has gone out to fight the robbers, and he wants you to change the baby into that great armed giant to help him. But don't you do it, for the baron will certainly be killed, there are so many robbers in that place. Please change the baby

"YOU ARE THE NOBLEST MAN," SAID LITZA.

into a very strong, fleet man who knows the country, and who will take the baron in his arms and bring him back here just as fast as he can."

"I will wish that," said the grandmother. And she did so. The baron had just arrived in sight of the robbers' stronghold, when he was very much surprised to find that, instead of carrying a baby in his arms, he himself was in the grasp of a tall, powerful man, who was carrying him at the top of his speed toward the town. The baron kicked and struggled much worse than the baby had, but the man paid no attention to his violent remonstrances, and soon set him down in the courtyard of the inn.

"This is your doing," he said to Litza. "I wished to show the prince that it was not fear that kept me from fighting the robbers, and you have prevented me."

"You have proved that you are brave," said Litza, "and that is enough. The prince is a bad man; let him fight his own robbers."

The baron could not be angry at this proof of Litza's prudent affection. And the next morning the party left the town on three horses, which the baron bought with one of his diamonds. The tall, fleet man who knew the country acted as guide, and led them by a by-road which did not pass near the School for Men. They arrived at the castle early on Christmas Eve, and the baron sent for his servants, his friends, and a priest, and he and Litza were married amid great rejoicing, for everybody was glad to see him come to his own again.

The next day Litza and the baron asked the grandmother to show them her magical servant in his original form. The old woman called the tall, fleet guide, and transformed him into the Green Goblin of the Third Word. This strange creature wildly danced and skipped before them, and, taking a watermelon and three pumpkins from his pocket, he tossed them up, keeping two of them always in the air.

The baron and his wife were very much amused by the antics of the goblin, and Litza exclaimed: "Oh, grandmother, if I were you I would keep him this way always. He would be wonderfully amusing, and I am sure he could carry you about, and scare away robbers, and do ever so many things."

"A merry green goblin might suit you," said the old woman, shaking her head, "but it would not suit me. I want to return to my own little home, and what I now wish is a suitable companion."

Instantly the goblin changed into a healthy middle-aged woman of agreeable manners, and willing to make herself useful. With this "suitable companion" the old grandmother returned, after the holidays, to her much-loved cottage, where she was often visited by the young baron and his wife; but, although they sometimes asked it, she never let them see the green goblin again.

"When a circumstance is just as accommodating as you want it to be," she said, "the less you meddle with it the better."

THE GREAT SHOW IN KOBOL-LAND.

IN by-gone days, and in a distant land, there was a certain small kingdom called Tanobar, which was governed in a manner not altogether satisfactory to the people. About ten years before the beginning of this story there had sat upon the throne two kings who, being twin brothers, had an equal right to rule. Being men of good disposition, and of much the same mind, they had for many years governed the country to the satisfaction of everybody.

When these twin kings died, within a few days of each other, one left a son about twelve years old and the other a daughter of the same age. The queen mothers, both estimable women, reigned as regents until their children came of age. And now, for more than a year, the two young people had sat upon the throne, and worn the crowns of the twin kings, their fathers.

Chamian was the name of the young king, and Millice, that of his cousin, the queen. It was the hope of all who desired the good of the country that these two should marry, and thus form a united government, but it did not seem probable that this would ever happen. The cousins were of very different dispositions, and although they had not yet quarrelled, or violently opposed each other, there was no sympathy between them, and one seldom approved of what the other did.

Chamian was a bold, active, and athletic fellow, and delighted in field sports and all sorts of out-door life, while Millice was of an intellectual turn of mind, and devoted to the study of art and science. During the time that these two had governed, no ques-

THE TWIN KINGS.

tions of public importance had arisen, but it was feared that if it should be necessary for the government to take any decided action it would be difficult to make the cousins agree upon a course. If the two should marry there would probably be no further cause for anxiety, for the queen would naturally defer to the king, and all would go on smoothly; but, as has been said before, for this happy issue there was no reason to hope.

But there was one man in Tanobar who did not desire the cousins to marry; who did not desire the government to go on smoothly, and whose earnest purpose was to effect a general revolution in public affairs, in order that he might reconstruct them to suit his own plans. This man was named Gromline, and he was the Minister of Agriculture. He was a man of great ability and very much given to stirring up political dissensions, and the principal reason for making him Minister of Agriculture had been that it was thought that in that department he could do no mischief. But since he had occupied this position he had come very near inflicting upon the country what most sensible people thought would be a terrible injury.

He had discovered a plant, which, after years of experiment and culture, he had now brought to what he considered perfection. This plant he named the Cosmic Bean, for the reason that it was capable of taking the place of all other food, and becoming the universal nutriment of mankind. Cooked in certain ways, it tasted like meats, and afforded the same nourishment. Prepared in other methods, it resembled different kinds of vegetables, bread, and even cheese and butter. It could be dried in various ways, and so used to make drinks resembling tea, coffee, and chocolate, and its juices when fermented produced several sorts of wines and spirits. In fact, there was no article of common food for which an excellent substitute could not be produced from the Cosmic Bean.

A most important property of this plant was that it would grow in any soil, with little or no cultivation, and that it was an evergreen, and produced its fruits in great abundance all the year round. Gromline's experiments and exhibitions had satisfied the government that his bean would do everything that he claimed for it, and that it might, indeed, take the place of all other food.

But from the wise people of the country Gromline's efforts to introduce his bean had met with the most decided opposition. It had not been brought to perfection during the lives of the twin kings, but they had both declared that should Gromline ever succeed in his efforts, the plant ought to be immediately eradicated from the face of the earth. Their wives, the queens regent, were of the same opinion, and when the Cosmic Bean was ready for cultivation and introduction, had forbidden Gromline or anybody else to grow it, and had ordered the destruction of all plants, wherever found. The young king and queen had done nothing, so far, in regard to the matter. Neither of them took any interest in beans or in Gromline.

The reasons urged against the production of the new food were very good ones. If this were a plant capable of giving people, old and young, all the different sorts of nutriment they needed or cared for, and which would grow everywhere without trouble to anybody and yield fruit in abundance at all seasons, it was quite certain that a great part of the people of the country would be content to let nature provide for them and to cease to provide for themselves. If all persons could live comfortably who chose to do a little work for themselves, nobody would do any work for anybody else. This state of affairs, as the officers of the government plainly saw, would soon turn everything upside down; the upper classes would soon cease to be upper if the lower classes ceased to work for them, and so this mischievous Cosmic Bean must be suppressed and, if possible, annihilated.

Gromline knew as well as any one what might happen if he

succeeded in making it possible for every man to be as lazy as he pleased, but he still persevered in his purpose. If he could introduce his universal food the greater part of the people in the country would look upon him as a benefactor, accept him as a leader, and perhaps make him their king. If he should succeed in putting himself on the throne he knew how to treat people who would not work for him. He had discovered a blight for the Cosmic Bean!

Since the accession of the new king and queen Gromline had made no progress in his plans, and he was getting very impatient. The worst thing that could happen to him would be for these two to marry. In that case all would probably go on as before, and he would have no chance. But if each of the two were to marry some outsider, there would be two royal families, dissensions must soon follow, and these would give him the opportunity to work out his own plans.

Not knowing what to do, Gromline went to a sorcerer to ask advice. The old gentleman listened to the case with great attention.

"I see your point," said he, when the minister had finished. "Did you ever happen to consider, in this connection, Prince Atto and the Princess Lista?"

"Never thought of them!" exclaimed Gromline.

"Well, sir," said the sorcerer, "I believe these two will answer your purpose in every respect. Nustyria, their miserable, stony country, adjoins this. Their parents will be glad for them to marry anybody who will have them. Lista is a wild, harum-scarum, horsy and doggy girl, who would enter gladly into all the pursuits of the king, and Atto is a thin-legged, round-shouldered bookworm, who devotes himself to the very things that please Queen Millice. More than this, these two hate each other heartily, and if they married our sovereigns the dissensions you desire would come on quickly enough."

"Admirable!" cried Gromline. "Those two youngsters are just the couple I want, but the king and queen have never seen them. The two nations are not friendly, and how will it be possible to bring these young people together?"

The sorcerer considered. "The simplest thing will be," he said, "to have them meet on neutral ground. What do you think of getting some sort of a show in the lower part of Kobol-land, in the Dimmer-Glade, for instance, which lies near both countries? If you make it attractive in the proper way, I have no doubt that our king and queen, as well as Prince Atto and Princess Lista, will be sure to attend it."

Gromline waved his hat around his head. "You hit the mark," he cried, "and I know exactly what I shall do. I will get up a great flower show, and in connection with it there shall be athletic sports. Queen Millice adores flowers, and so does that young Atto. The sports will bring the other two, and in Kobol-land we can do as we please. No laws can interfere with us there. I

"GRAGLICK, MEASURE MY GRIN."

shall exhibit my bean. My friend, I owe you everlasting gratitude."

"And seventy sequins," said the sorcerer.

When the Minister of Agriculture had departed, the sorcerer sat and smiled and smiled and smiled. His amusement was so great that it impressed itself upon his attention, and he summoned his body servant.

"Graglick," said he, "measure my grin."

Taking a tape measure from his pocket, the servant obeyed.

"Master," he said, "it is eight inches and a quarter long."

"Ha!" exclaimed the sorcerer, "that is my largest grin, and well might it be. I shall have a fine joke on this fellow with his Cosmic Bean, and his schemes for revolution. This royal matchmaker and throne-upsetter! A flower show and athletic sports in Kobol-land! Oh, there will be rare times!"

The sorcerer had good cause for expecting rare times. Kobol-land, which, at its southern extremity, touched the two kingdoms, extended far away into the unknown regions, and was the home of fairies, gnomes, giants, genii, afrits, centaurs, nymphs, dryads, brownies, dragons, griffins, and other wonderful and curious beings. Few people from either of the adjoining countries ever wandered far into Kobol-land. But the Dimmer-Glade, a beautiful region, scarcely a mile from the southern boundary, had frequently been visited by parties who were fond of lovely scenery and took an interest in the strange inhabitants of the place, who, even those with terrible aspects, had always been friendly enough to occasional visitors.

There could be no doubt that a great show, a short distance within the borders of Kobol-land, would attract a vast crowd of strangers of both high and low degree, and not only that—and the sorcerer laughed aloud as he thought of it—such an exhibition would draw to it every queer creature of the land, from the biggest giant to the smallest pigwidgeon, and if this rare mixture of exhibitors and spectators at a flower show, and of competitors in athletic games, did not result in a high old time it would be wonderful indeed.

But the sorcerer had hopes that the show would have far more important results than the fun, the excitement, and the surprising occurrences which might be expected at a great concourse, where visitors from ordinary countries would mingle on common ground with the strange inhabitants of Kobol-land. He thought he had reason to believe that something of advantage to his country would result from this exhibition.

The sorcerer was a good sort of man, and knowing that the Minister of Agriculture was a most dangerous plotter against the public welfare, he was delighted to think that he had proposed a plan the influence and effect of which would probably be exactly the opposite to those for which Gromline was scheming.

On the next day after the conversation between Gromline and the sorcerer the whole kingdom of Tanobar was gorgeous with many-colored placards announcing the great show in Kobol-land, and very shortly afterward the walls and trees of Nustyria were decorated with like brilliant placards, which the Minister of Agriculture sent over the border by the wagon-load.

The announcement created great interest and excitement, and early on the opening day nearly everybody in the two countries who was able to do so was on the road to the Dimmer-Glade. People on horses, people in wagons, people on camels, elephants, and on foot, with here and there a man bestriding an ox or an ostrich, crowded the highways and byways leading to Kobol-land.

King Chamian, on a tail hunter, rode boldly thither with a little band of courtiers and companions, while, in a handsome carriage, drawn by four cream-colored horses, and followed by other carriages containing the ladies of her court, the young Queen Millice journeyed to the flower show.

From the capital of Nustyria came the Princess Lista on a wiry bob-tailed steed, with wicked back-turned ears, and a pace so swift

THE JOURNEY TO KOBOL-LAND.

that her attendants were left behind long before she reached the Dimmer-Glade. And from that city came also the Prince Atto, stretched at full length on a cushioned platform, borne on the back of an elephant, and busily engaged in the study of a book of logarithms, while an attendant crouched by him and held a sun umbrella over his head.

The desire of this Princess and this Prince of Nustyria to visit the show in Kobol-land had been greatly increased when they heard that King Chamian and Queen Millice would be there. Although Atto and Lista belonged to a royal family they were not heirs to the throne of Nustyria, and having but very poor prospects in their native land would be very glad to make marriages which would bring them good positions and fortunes, and what could suit them better than alliances with the noble young King and beautiful young Queen of Tanobar?

Lista had never met Chamian, but she had heard of his deeds of horsemanship and athletics, and felt certain he was just the sort of man she would like, while Atto knew all about Millice and was quite as sure that she would suit him as he was that she could not find a better husband than himself.

Of the possibilities of a divided kingdom the prince and princess thought not at all, and, in fact, they gave very little thought to each other; and, when they did, Atto wished that the king and Lista might break their necks together, and Lista said to herself that if Atto would travel away with Queen Millice, or with anybody else, and go so far that she would never see him again, she would be very glad indeed.

Arrived at the Dimmer-Glade, the visitors found there a grand pavilion erected for the flower show, while booths and tents of various sizes and colors decorated the grassy plain. A wide stretch of level land at the upper end of the glade, and nearly surrounded by low hills, on which thousands of spectators could sit or stand, was set aside for the athletic games. As the show was to last three days, kings, queens, princes, princesses, rich people and poor ones pitched their tents far up and down the smooth expanse of the Dimmer-Glade.

Although the news of the show had created a great popular

sensation throughout Tanobar and Nustyria, the excitement among the inhabitants of Kobol-land was even greater. The affair was so novel and promised to be so interesting that even the mighty giant Jirg, who seldom came out of his lofty castle, except to hunt in the wild mountains of the north, declared his intention of attending the show. From the mysterious labyrinths of the dark gorges came afrits, black, shiny, and with stealthy tread. And from the mines and the hills crept many a gnome, wondering what he was going to see.

As to fairies, there was no end to them. The queen and her court were there, and nearly all her subjects. A troop of dryads took possession of a grove of oak-trees near the glade, and among some high rocks at the head of a quiet little lake four sirens ensconced themselves with their harps.

As many of the Kobol-landers intended to exhibit in the flower show and compete in the games, these mixed freely with the other exhibitors and the visitors, and it was not long before a general air of sociability pervaded the glade.

Queen Millice was in her royal tent sipping a cup of chocolate

ALL FAIRYLAND WAS THERE.

when suddenly the tent was filled with a sort of smoky fog, so dense that she could see nothing about her. Supposing that the furniture had taken fire she was about to cry out for assistance, when the vapor resolved itself into the form of a tall genie, who seated himself upon the divan, crossed his legs, and with a bland smile inquired how she liked the country.

As this individual had never been presented to her, and for other reasons, the young queen hesitated a little before entering into conversation; but remembering where she was, and that this was one of the natives of the soil, she replied with her usual courtesy, and the two were soon engaged in a pleasant chat. The genie was curious to know if this was her first visit to Kobol-land, and how long she intended to stay, and with much animation he told her of points of great interest which she should not fail to visit before leaving.

The queen of the fairies paid a royal visit to Chamian, and he was so delighted with her that he said to some of his courtiers that if she were bigger, or he were smaller, he would give up his throne and ask to be made king of the fairies.

Princess Lista rode directly to Chamian's stables, where she found a company of brownies, combing and brushing the horses till they shone like silk. This greatly pleased Lista, and she was about to offer the brownies a permanent engagement in her stables, but on second thought she concluded to wait and see how things turned out.

Prince Atto had always doubted the existence of griffins, but walking near the flower pavilion he beheld one of these great creatures descending from the upper air, and holding between its fore paws a large pot of chrysanthemums. Swooping down close to him the griffin said to Atto:

"Will you be so good, sir, as to take hold of one side of this pot, so that I can set it on the ground without shaking the earth or injuring the flowers?"

Atto had never been asked to help anybody to do any sort of work, and his princely soul instantly rebelled at this request, but after a second look at the griffin he took hold of one side of the pot and helped the winged monster to set it gently on the ground.

When the flower pavilion was opened it was soon filled with an animated crowd. The display of flowers and plants was so curious and wonderful that even Chamian and Lista, who usually cared little for such things, were greatly interested. The first thing that met the eyes of the people as they came in at the grand entrance was a double row of plants of the Cosmic Bean, brought from Gromline's secret gardens.

The ripe beans, which, mingled with the blossoms and pods in all stages of growth, hung in astonishing profusion from the tall plants, were freely offered to the visitors. And as these had a delicious flavor when eaten raw, the people were delighted with them, and eagerly read the great placards on which were printed the wonderful virtues and advantages of the Cosmic Bean.

Around the great central space of the pavilion, and up and down its long passageways, was arranged a collection of plants such as never before had been seen in this world.

The plants contributed by the Kobol-landers were far more curious than any others. The chrysanthemum brought by the griffin occupied a conspicuous place. Its flowers were as large as saucers and of a blood-red color. Whenever the plant was watered streaks of fiery yellow shot through the petals, and a shower of little sparks was thrown off in every direction. This chrysanthemum was labelled Miss Sophia Hypogrif.

There was a very odd cactus, which was exhibited by two brownies, who had taken years to bring it to perfection. Every quarter of an hour a bud appeared on one of the leaves of this cactus, and this bud grew and swelled for about two minutes, when it opened and displayed a large cucumber pickle, ready to eat.

In a circular tank was a water lily, exhibited by an elderly mermaid. The leaves of the lily, which were large and lay flat upon the water, were very hot, so that food could be cooked upon them, particularly griddle cakes, which were made in great numbers by some little black imps, who took a keen delight in serving them to the visitors who surrounded the tank. The mermaid herself never ate griddle cakes, which might be inferred from the fact that she was elderly.

The fairies contributed a great number of beautiful flowers, among which were the convertible blossoms. A bud on one of these plants would open and disclose a rose. In an hour this would change to a marigold, in another hour to a chrysanthemum. It would then become a zinnia, a tulip, and so change hourly into other flowers, until at the twelfth transformation it became an immortelle and lasted indefinitely.

There was a species of dogwood, grown principally by afrits, the long branches of which were trained to hang close to the ground and catch rats.

There were blossoms like great sunflowers, each of which revolved on a pivot, and dazzled the eyes of the beholders; there were egg-plants, the fruit of which could be hatched in the sun, and produced different sorts of barnyard fowls; and there was the "ghost-plant," misty and vaporous to the view, through the leaves and stems of which one might pass his hand without injury to the plant. There was the "tourist vine," which, growing under a tree, would send up a long shoot until it reached a lower branch. Fastening itself to this, it would suddenly contract and pull itself up by the roots; these would be drawn up and attached to the limb, and the plant would again send up its shoot, reach a higher limb, and draw itself up as before. In this way it would climb to the top of the tree, where, attaching its roots to the topmost branch, it would send its shoot high into the air, where it would seize on the first large bird that passed near enough, and, loosening its root from the tree, would be carried to a foreign land.

There were talking flowers which said, "good morning," "papa," "mamma"; there were flowers contributed by the demon of the glacier, which looked like roses and dahlias and other blossoms, but were really water-ices of delicious flavors, which, when plucked for eating, would quickly be succeeded by others upon the same stems. Besides these unnatural and curious plants there could be seen in this show every sort of ordinary flower, the size, fragrance, and beauty of which had been so improved that it could scarcely be recognized.

King Chamian and Lista soon became, of course, good friends, and wandered together through the pavilion; and, although they could not fail to be amused at the curious and wonderful plants they saw, they were impatient for the afternoon and the beginning of the sports.

Millice walked by herself, followed by some of her ladies and watched by Atto, who intended to make himself known to her, but wished to wait a little in order to find out what sort of a girl she was. Gromline was near by, and, seeing that the queen and Prince Atto were not likely to become acquainted, hastened to Atto, led him to Millice, and presented him. The queen and the prince had walked together but a short distance when they came upon a plant contributed by a Nustyrian gardener, which rivalled some of the productions of the Kobol-landers. He had grafted the water-lily, the sugar-cane, the cow-tree, and the fire-weed upon a tea-plant, and when one of the large, cup-like blossoms was pulled off and held under the end of the broken stem, it was speedily filled with fragrant and delicious tea. Although Millice did not care for many of the monstrosities she had seen, this plant attracted her, and Atto was also interested in it, for he was fond of tea. After drinking two cups of the beverage, an idea struck him.

"Would you like a plant like this, Queen Millice?"

"I should like it very much. I wonder if the seed can be procured?"

"The plant itself would be much better," said Atto, and, turning to the gardener, he inquired the price.

"One hundred sequins, your highness," replied the man.

"Nonsense," said the prince; "twenty-five will be quite enough. I will take the plant, and you can have it carried immediately to my tent."

"But, your highness," said the poor man, turning a little pale, "I have spent more than that upon it, and besides, it would injure me very much to have it removed from exhibition at the very beginning of the flower show. Without this plant my collection is nothing."

"Take it to my tent," said Atto, who wished to put a pretty inscription on it and send it to the queen. "You have to be very careful with these fellows," he said, turning to Millice, "or they will cheat you dreadfully."

The young queen answered not a word, but stepping backward, called one of her ladies, and with her walked away, leaving Atto standing by himself. The prince was a good deal disconcerted by this proceeding, and after gazing a few minutes after Millice, he said to the gardener that he could leave the plant where it was for the present, as he might not want it; and then walked away to consider the situation.

"I have made a mistake," he said to himself. "I have shown

her, too abruptly, my habits of prudence and economy. I must do something to make a good impression upon her."

By this time he had reached one of the doors of the pavilion, and he stepped into the open air. At the end of the glade he saw the most lively preparations going on for the games in the afternoon. Even now the people were leaving the pavilion and flocking to the hills to secure good places. At one of the best points for observation he saw that there had been erected two royal stands.

"Aha!" said he to himself, "the queen intends to view the games. It might be well if I were to take a part in them. Women, even the best of them, are so foolish as to like that sort of thing. But the trouble is, I don't know how to do anything athletic. I have never engaged in such fatiguing and senseless exercises. But nearly everybody will be doing something, and I do not like to be left out."

At this moment he heard a sound like a great wind behind him, and quickly turning he saw the griffin swooping to the ground.

"I am glad to see you again, young man," said the monster. "You were very kind to help me with that flower-pot, so that I did not injure a blossom of my chrysanthemums, which will probably get the prize. I should like to do something for you. I suppose you are going to take part in the games. How would you like to ride me bareback around the arena? That is a great chance for a young man, and one seldom offered."

Atto trembled in every fibre.

"Oh, I could never do that!" he exclaimed; "I cannot ride bareback even on a horse, and it would be impossible on anything flying through the air."

"Nonsense," said the griffin; "it is as easy and as safe as winking. You can stand on my back."

"Stand?" cried Atto, in horror.

"Yes," said the monster, "you will find that even more secure than sitting, and it will make a much better show. I will curl my tail high over my back, and make it as stiff as a bar of iron. My horny lumps will give you a good footing, and with your hands firmly grasping the upper end of my tail, it will be impossible for you to fall off. Good! The thing is settled! I was looking for some one to ride me, and you are the very man. You are not heavy and I want to do you a favor. I will go now and arrange for our performance, and at the proper time I will look you up."

So saying, the griffin surged away through the air, and poor Atto remained, shaking in his boots.

"Here will be a blood-curdling way of appearing before the queen," he thought. "And there's no getting out of it; that winged monster will be sure to look me up!"

GROMLINE AND HIS BEAN.

Gromline was in a very good humor; his plans appeared to be working admirably. Everybody was talking about his Cosmic Bean, and even the Princess Lista, who usually paid little attention to such things, had said that she wished it could be introduced into her country, and then, perhaps, there might be less said about the starving poor.

Moreover, King Chamian and Lista were getting acquainted very fast, and he had invited her to sit in his royal box when she was not taking part in the games. This was all very well. If these two should marry there would be a great chance for him and his bean, but in regard to Queen Millice things were not going on so well; she had soon separated herself from Prince Atto, and was now sitting alone in her box reading a book until the games should begin. The prince had not been invited to sit with her, that was plain to see.

This was not all satisfactory to Gromline, but it did not dampen his spirits. It could scarcely be expected that grave and studious people like Millice and Atto could come together as quickly as the more lively Chamian and Lista. But if the prince had any sense or wit at all, he could not fail to make an impression upon Millice before the show was over.

The games were just about to begin when Gromline met Atto. "What is the matter with your highness?" the minister exclaimed. "Are you not feeling well?"

"Not very," replied Atto, and in the hope that Gromline might be able to help him he told him of the proposition of the griffin.

"I am afraid," said the prince, "to absolutely refuse his offer, for if he is made angry there is no knowing what he may do. Can you think of any way in which I can get out of this scrape?"

"Get out of it!" cried Gromline. "Don't dream of such a

thing. Here is a chance of performing an astounding and unheard-of feat without the least danger in the world. It will not do for you to lose it. It will impress everybody, especially Queen Millice, with the conviction that, although a prince of intellect does not in general care for useless sports, still, when he pleases, he can with ease perform a feat far above anything which the athletes have even thought of."

Poor Atto sighed. It appeared that he was in for it.

The games began with a hurdle footrace, open to all competitors. Among those who ran were stout-legged young men from Tanobar and Nustyria, three youthful giants from the mountains—who were, however, too heavy to jump, and broke down several hurdles—a lot of nimble brownies, and many other two-legged Kobol-landers. A genie, with blazing eyes, soon took the lead, often going over two hurdles at once, although they were a considerable distance apart, but he was ruled out of the race because his soaring flights were neither running nor jumping. Near the head of the long line was the sorcerer's kangaroo, who at one time made a beautiful bound entirely over a Nustyrian athlete, who at that moment was clearing a hurdle, but he was also ruled out of the race because he did nothing but jump, and did not run at all.

There were others who did not understand the rules, and among these were several gnomes of the mines, with long beards and spindle legs, who ran with great swiftness but went under the hurdles without so much as bobbing their heads, never imagining that they were expected to jump over those lofty bars. An afrit won this race, his long, black, shining body bounding and darting ahead like an India-rubber savage dipped in oil.

Next came a grand horserace, in which each steed was to be ridden by its owner. And in this King Chamian and Princess

Lista took part. The young king rode a black courser of the desert; the princess was mounted on her raw-boned mare, all fire and muscle, with wicked eyes and back-bent ears. There were about fifty other steeds, mounted by all sorts of riders. Among these was a lively sprite bestriding a Pegasus colt, but he was not allowed to enter the race, because it was quite certain that his horse would use his wings. The sprite was greatly grieved by this decision, and said he was perfectly willing that all the other riders should put up sails if that would make things even. Another rider was a ghost who had formerly been a celebrated horseman, but he soon came to grief, for his horse, imagining that no one was on his back, kicked up his heels and tossed himself entirely through the body of his rider, and, flirting his tail through the separated portion, dashed to one side and left the course.

Chamian rode splendidly, and his swift horse soon carried him to the head of the line, but Lista was beside him, and her wicked mare with glaring eyes, who sped faster and faster as her blood grew hotter, soon took the lead and kept it till the race was done, and the shouts of the multitude proclaimed her the victor.

Queen Millice had watched this race with much interest, for she liked to see the fine action of a spirited horse, and she was very sorry that Lista's ugly beast had won the race. She would have been much better pleased if her cousin's beautiful charger had been the winner, not because he belonged to Chamian, but because he was such a noble animal.

The princess was very proud of her victory, and her heart beat high at the congratulations which poured in on her from every side.

"I have a colt at home," she cried to Chamian, "who is more fiery and wicked than this mare, with better withers, pasterns, hocks and cannon bones, and I am going to train him so that I can outdo even what I have done to-day," and she laughed triumphantly.

King Chamian did not very much like to be beaten, but as he was beaten he was glad that it was Lista, and no one else, who had come in ahead of him. She was a fine, spirited horse-woman, and he liked that sort of a girl, but he could not help wishing that she did not laugh and talk quite so loudly, and did not speak so familiarly to her grooms.

There now trotted into the arena a handsome centaur, both his man part and his horse part denoting high breeding. He approached the royal boxes, and bowed to the occupants. Queen Millice was pleased with the courteous air and the graceful movements of the centaur, and was curious to know what he was going to do. She beckoned him toward her.

"Have you no competitors?" she asked.

"None, your majesty," replied the centaur, with a bow and a smile, "excepting old Father Time."

"I do not understand," said Millice.

"It is my intention, your majesty," explained the centaur, "to trot alone around this arena, and to endeavor to beat any previous record of fast time; and not only this, but to make such a record for myself as cannot easily be beaten in the future."

The queen was very much interested in the effort the centaur was about to make in this race against his ancestors and his posterity—she liked a high ambition.

"What is the quickest time a mile has yet been trotted in?" she asked.

"Two minutes and eight and a quarter seconds," replied the centaur, "and by your majesty's permission, I will now endeavor to beat that." And with a bow, which he repeated as he passed the other royal box, the centaur began to trot around the ring, so as to warm himself for his work.

He did not go very fast at first, but when he reached the starting post he set off at a great pace. His legs moved beneath him with such rapidity that they could scarcely be seen, and his body shook and trembled as if a steam-engine were working at its highest velocity inside of him.

Around he went, the spectators almost holding their breaths as he passed, until he shot by the judges' stand, and slackened his speed. In an instant one of the judges dashed at a tall blackboard, and marked upon it, in great figures, two minutes and seven and three-quarters seconds. The centaur had beaten all previous records.

Then went up a great shout from the multitude, and for a time nothing could be heard but cheering and clapping. Lista and Chamian came down from their box, and shook the centaur by the hand, while Queen Millice beckoned to him to approach her. Pushing through the crowd that surrounded him, and wiping his heated face with his handkerchief, the centaur came to the queen's box.

"You have done well," said she. "I congratulate you on your success."

The centaur bowed and thanked her.

"But it is only half a success," he said. "It is true I have beaten the past, but I must now trot against coming ages."

Again the track was cleared, and the centaur prepared for his second heat. This time he held a stop-watch in his hand, so that he might see as he trotted how fast he was going, and, if necessary, increase his efforts. Away he sped, and at the half-mile post he held up his watch before him, and then all could see that his wonderful speed was increased.

If it had seemed before that a steam-engine were working within him, one might now imagine that same engine had broken loose from all government, and was tearing him to pieces as it hurled him forward. The people's eyes could scarcely move fast enough to follow him. The judges were pale with excitement as he passed their stand, and then high on the blackboard, where every one could see them, were inscribed the figures 1.59¼.

With a wild yell of delight the whole audience prepared to rush toward the centaur, and in a moment he would have been embraced and perhaps smothered by hundreds of enthusiastic spectators, but dashing to the queen's box he stopped only long enough to say:

"That, your majesty, is for posterity to beat," and then galloped away out of the reach of the roaring multitude.

The Minister of Agriculture had been watching Millice, and was greatly pleased to see the interest she had taken in the centaur.

"Things go even better than I thought they would," he said to himself; "it could hardly be expected that at a time like this, when everything is in such a lively hubbub, she and Atto could have a chance to get interested in each other's ideas about books and education; but if she likes the trotting of that man-horse, she is bound to care ever so much more for the daring and courage of a prince who rides a bare-backed griffin. I never imagined that Atto would have such a chance as that to ingratiate himself with our queen. Truly, I am having most excellent luck."

At that moment Gromline espied the griffin, who, with his wings folded, was hurrying here and there along the outskirts of the crowd, evidently looking for some one.

"Do you know," said the monster, coming up to the minister, "where I can find Prince Atto? Our great mid-air performance is set down for this afternoon, but it strikes me that the little coward has run away. But I must find him if I can, for it will be a great thing for me to go through the act with a blooded prince on my back."

"Indeed it will," said Gromline, "and it will be a great thing for him, too. I would advise you by no means to perform without him, and I will go now and help you look for him."

Prince Atto had not seen much of the performance in the arena, for he had been busily and anxiously engaged endeavoring to find some one who would act as his substitute in the griffin performance. Every one to whom he made the proposal declined with the greatest promptness. But a mischievous imp of the hot springs, who overheard the prince endeavoring to bribe an afrit with two bunches of bananas, offered himself as a rider, and said he would do the job for a bottle of ink and a squirt gun; but Atto knew the griffin would never accept such a substitute as that, and so, in great perplexity and apprehension, continued his search. He would have been glad to hide himself till night and then hurry back to his home, but he knew this would not help him. An angry griffin could find him as well in Nustyria as anywhere else.

Hurrying on, and scarcely knowing where he was going, Atto found himself on the shores of a lake, and moored close by he saw a little boat. This pleased him; he was tired and warm, and to float over the smooth water would rest and revive him. He had not gone far when he heard the sound of sweet voices singing, and the music of harps. Looking in the direction of the sounds he saw four beautiful sirens on the top of some high rocks. Atto was fond of music, and rowed near the rocks.

As Prince Atto approached the rocks, the sirens, who had not seen a person upon the lake that day, everybody having gone to the show and the races, were greatly pleased and animated, and they sung more sweetly and touched their harps more melodiously. Atto, who had given up all hopes of finding a substitute, and expected every moment to hear the griffin rushing through the air in quest of him, thought he might as well enjoy himself while he had a chance, and rested on his oars as he listened to this charming music.

But this did not suit the sirens. They wanted him to come nearer, so that his boat might be wrecked upon the rocks. They sung the most delightful love songs, in which they called him by name, and tenderly reproached him for refusing them his delightful society. But Atto smiled, and shook his head. He had read about sirens and shipwrecked sailors, and he was not going to be caught in their trap. But he was quite willing to enjoy what might be called a free concert, and so kept at a safe distance and listened with great satisfaction.

After a time the fair singers perceived that their songs would never lure this wary youth upon the rocks, and their music ceased. The prince now began to row away, but the sirens did not intend to let him off so easily. One of them leaned over the rocks, and called to him.

"Fair prince," said she, "one moment stay, we pray you. We have heard of your great learning and of your quick wit, and we had hoped, by our songs, to draw you near to us, so that we might put to you a question which has greatly puzzled us, and since we have first heard it, has kept us awake night after night. We believe you to be the only one in all this region who can solve this problem for us, and we humbly pray you to listen to it and give us the answer."

This interested Prince Atto. He was proud of his ability to work out problems, and was always willing to show it, so he stopped and then rowed a little nearer to the rocks.

"What do you want to know?" he said; "speak plainly, and I can hear it at this distance."

"The puzzle we wish you to solve for us is this," said the siren who had before spoken. "I am composed of four parts, but represent one thousand five hundred and fifty-one separate portions. My first part is far greater than the other three, but my second is as good as any one. My first will go twice as far as my last, twenty times as far as my third, and yet my second can see farther than all the rest put together. My third is the square root of double my first, plus my fourth. My whole is soft and gentle, and yet my second and third have only to change places, and there is a falsehood in my very centre."

Atto's eyes sparkled as he heard this puzzle.

"That is truly difficult," said he, "but I think I can work it out for you," and so saying he drew in his oars, and took a piece of paper and a pencil from his pocket.

"Tell it to me again," he said to the siren, "and I will write it down; then in a few minutes I will give you the answer."

The siren obeyed, and the prince went to work on the puzzle. He worked and worked and worked, but he found the problem a good deal harder than he had expected it to be, and the time passed rapidly without his knowing it. As he sat completely absorbed in his occupation, one of the sirens took the wire strings from her harp and, after fastening them together, made a little hook in one end of this cord, which she deftly threw into the bow of the boat without Atto perceiving it. Then, very gently, she began to pull him toward the rocks, the other sirens breathlessly watching her operations. If they could wreck and drown the prince, it would be the rarest fun for them.

The slender cord was drawn in so gradually that Atto did not feel the motion of the boat, which slowly but surely approached some sharp points of rock, which could not fail to penetrate the delicate and fragile bottom of this little bark.

But the sport of the sirens was not unobserved; the company of dryads who had taken up their quarters in the oak grove near by, and who had not ventured among the crowds at the races, although they had all seen the flower show, had watched with much interest the solitary boatman on the lake and had been greatly concerned for his safety when they found that the sirens were endeavoring to allure him to destruction. It had delighted them to see that the prince was aware of his danger, and that he prudently kept away from the rocks; but now that the sirens were taking an undue advantage of him the dryads grew very angry, and gliding gently between the trees they approached the shore.

The siren had now drawn the boat so near the points of rock that a strong jerk would knock it against them, and her eyes and those of her sisters were glistening with the anticipation of the delightful scene which would follow. But one of the dryads, running ahead of the others, sprang behind the siren who held the cord, and gave her a vigorous push, which sent her headlong into the water.

Atto, startled by the great splash, turned quickly, and imagining that the sirens were jumping into the lake to capture him by main force, he seized the oars and pulled rapidly to a safe distance, and then stopped.

"Heigho!" he cried, as the unfortunate siren rose to the surface, and began to swim toward the shore; "what is the meaning of all this?"

The sirens themselves scarcely knew what had happened, for every dryad was now behind a tree; but they called to the prince that he need not be frightened; one of their sisters had accidentally fallen into the water, that was all, and they besought him to come back, and tell them the answer to the puzzle. But Atto believed that the siren had tried to jump into his boat, and he would not again approach the rocks. Turning around he began to row toward the place where he had found the boat.

"Come back, come back," the sirens screamed angrily after him, "and tell us the answer to our puzzle. You have no right to cheat us of it." Atto stopped rowing for a moment, and called back.

"I have the answer," he cried, "and it is very different from you, for it is the word 'mild,' and you are anything but mild," and laughing at them he quickly pulled ashore.

It was dark when Prince Atto reached his tent.

"Those sirens were really of great service to me," he said to himself, "for not only did they give me a very interesting puzzle, but they kept me out of the way till the games were over. I suppose the griffin found some one else to ride him, and I hope he has forgotten all about me."

That evening there was a grand display of fireworks, and this consisted entirely of the performance of ten or twelve fiery dragons, who flew through the air around and around, darting upward and downward and in every direction, all the time shooting showers of sparks and jets of flame from their nostrils, while their red-hot tails described fantastic figures in the air. It was a great scene. The whole Dimmer-Glade was lighted up by the sparks and flames of the swooping, snorting monsters as they circled overhead.

Everybody was out of doors, and Prince Atto stood by his tent, greatly impressed by the exhibition. Presently he heard his name called, and turning his eyes from the sky to the earth, he beheld the griffin standing by him.

"Fine show, isn't it?" said the winged creature. "It's a great success, and they are going to do it again to-morrow night. That big dragon up there, the one whose tail glows brightest, and who shoots sparks in every direction at once, will vary the performance to-morrow by carrying a man on his back. The man is to hold a great bouquet, and the dragon will keep the flowers lighted up all the time he is flying. I have recommended you for the rider. It is a great idea. A prince on a firework! Such a thing was never seen before, and will probably never be seen again."

Atto could not say a word. A chill went down his back, and his legs gave way beneath him, so that he sat suddenly upon the ground.

"Of course," continued the griffin, "if you should perform your bare-backed feat with me to-morrow afternoon you would be too tired to ride the dragon in the evening, and it would not be expected of you."

"Didn't you perform to-day?" gasped Atto.

"Oh, no," replied the griffin "I wouldn't be so mean as to go through that act without you, unless you would prefer the evening performance."

"Oh, no, no, no!" cried Atto, "I would rather ride you. I prefer that, I assure you."

"Very well, then," said the griffin, "be ready at five o'clock."

The next morning Atto met Gromline, and told him what had happened.

"I beg you will not trifle with that griffin again," said the Minister. "I never saw such an angry monster as he was yesterday afternoon, when it became necessary to postpone his act, because you could not be found. If I had not pacified him by ordering the judges of the flower show to give him a first prize for his chrysanthemum, there is no knowing what violent act he might have committed, so do not fail to be on hand to-day."

"You may be sure I shall not," Atto answered, dolefully. "He spoke gently to me, but I could see the fire in his eyes."

During the morning Queen Millice again visited the flower show, where she met King Chamian, who was selecting a bouquet for the Princess Lista.

"Are you going to take part in the sports to-day?" she asked him.

"Oh, yes," he replied, "this afternoon is to be devoted to games of strength and agility."

"If you do engage in these contests," said Millice, "I hope you will not allow yourself to be beaten. You rode well yesterday, but I did not like to see you come in second best."

"Why, cousin!" exclaimed Chamian, "I did not suppose you cared for such things."

"I care very much for the honor of the family." said the young queen.

Shortly afterward Millice encountered Atto. He was in low spirits, but he brightened up a little when he saw her.

"I have a puzzle which I will put to you," said he; "I know you like puzzles, and this is a fresh one which I heard yesterday;" and then he went on, and told her the siren's puzzle.

Queen Millice was much interested, and asking Atto to repeat the puzzle, she sat down to solve it. In about fifteen minutes she succeeded.

"That is an excellent puzzle," said she; "do you know any more as good as it is?"

"Oh, yes," said Atto, "I have at least a dozen of them in a little book. I will bring it, and read them to you."

"I shall like that," said Millice. "I do not think I shall care for the game this afternoon, and if you will bring your book to my pavilion I will try and work out some of the puzzles."

Atto sighed. "I am afraid I cannot be with you at that time," he said; "I perform myself this afternoon. I ride a griffin bareback."

"You!" exclaimed Millice. "Is it possible that you not only devote yourself to intellectual pursuits but to physical exercises?"

"Oh, yes," said Atto, straightening himself, and putting on an air of conscious merit; "I give preference to the perfection of my mental powers, but as a matter of course, I do not neglect my physical development. However, I never forget that I am a prince, and when I perform in public, I choose an act which no one but myself would dare undertake."

As the young queen walked back to her tent she could not help comparing Chamian and Atto. Here was her cousin, caring only for bodily exercises, taking part in games with low-born competitors, and worse than all, coming out second best. On the other hand, Atto was not only a prince of intellect, but a man of most daring courage, willing to undertake an unheard-of feat. In these reflections she quite forgot the incident of the cup-of-tea plant.

The first part of the afternoon was devoted to athletic games, such as vaulting, long jumps, high jumps, trapeze, tight-rope performances and other gymnastic acts. In several of these King Chamian took part, and each time he entered the arena he looked at the box of Queen Millice to see if she were observing him. It was not necessary for him to look at his own box, in which Lista sat. She watched everything, and was generally more excited and clapped her hands louder than anybody else. The young king was determined that, if he could help it, Millice should not see him come out second best again. He had never before given any thought to her opinion, for he had never before had reason to suppose she cared whether he succeeded or failed in anything.

Thus animated, Chamian vaulted higher than anybody else, not a Kobol-lander, and in hurling a javelin at a mark he surpassed all competitors. Lista loudly applauded his success, and wanted to go into the arena and hurl a javelin herself, but he dissuaded her.

There was then a grand fencing match, in which a unicorn entered the ring and challenged all comers.

After this spirited animal, with his long, tapering horn, had disconcerted some of the best swordsmen of Nustyria and Tanobar, King Chamian entered the lists against him, and by the rapid and skilful play of his stout blade not only warded off all the attacks of the unicorn, but at last forced him to turn tail and fly. At this

DUEL BETWEEN THE KING AND THE UNICORN.

victory Queen Millice stood up, clapped her hands and waved her handkerchief. That was a contest fit for a king.

In some of the games Chamian took no part, and throwing the great hammer was one of these. There were many competitors entered in this game, but they did not all have a chance, for the giant Jirg swung and hurled the hammer with such force that it flew as far as the lake where the sirens sang, and then descended into the water with such a tremendous splash that the four sisters on the rocks were nearly frightened out of their wits, and the dryads in the grove above, who ran out from their tree trunks when they heard the great noise, were all well wet by the descending shower of drops.

The tug of war next followed, in which a great number of Kobol-landers took hold of one end of a long cable, and the athletes from Tanobar and Nustyria grasped the other. As this was a sort of international contest everybody was wildly excited over it. The Kobol-landers would, undoubtedly, have won the victory had it not been for the bright thought of a judge from Tanobar, who, seeing how matters were likely to go, hastily made out naturalization papers for three wild giants who had just arrived, and were standing among the spectators. When these great hairy fellows became citizens of Tanobar and seized the end of the rope the struggling mass of Kobol-landers were dragged over the dividing line in less that twenty seconds. It is needless to say that this judge obtained preferment.

When this exciting contest had been finished a mounted herald, clad in crimson and gold, rode into the arena, and after blowing his trumpet, proclaimed in a loud voice that the sports of the day would conclude with a grand performance in mid-air, in which the valiant and fearless Prince Atto of Nustyria would ride a bareback griffin. This announcement created a great sensation, for no one who knew Prince Atto had supposed that he was a man who would undertake such an unheard-of feat.

The prince now entered the arena, and bowed to the ladies in the two royal boxes. Then he approached Queen Millice, and asked her if he had her good wishes in his present perilous feat. He looked bold and determined enough, for Gromline had been with him all the morning, assuring him that it would be the easiest thing in the world to ride a quiet, careful griffin, who would assist him in every possible way to keep his position, and to feel at ease; and the minister had, furthermore, fortified and encouraged him by an excellent luncheon, composed entirely of Cosmic Beans, cooked and prepared in many different ways. The queen was pleased with his brave appearance, and gave him a silken scarf to wear as a token of her interest.

Now the sound of great wings was heard, and the griffin, swooping through the air, came down to the ground in front of the royal boxes. Then, curling his tail high over his back, he informed Prince Atto that he was ready to begin the act. Without hesitation the young man stepped on the horny back of the monster, and stood upright, steadying himself by holding fast to the stiffened tail.

Slowly uprose the great griffin into the air, Prince Atto standing upright on his back. This was not a difficult feat, nor an unsafe one, so long as the griffin's tail, by which Atto steadied himself, remained stiffly in position. As the first gentle circle above the arena was made, Atto looked a little pale, but he felt that his position was secure, and bowed and smiled as shouts of applause came up from the great multitude.

This griffin was a monster of a very hot and revengeful disposition, and his anger against Atto for deserting him and preventing his performance on the first day had not in the least cooled, and although his manner toward the young man had been very mild, he had determined that, during this act, he would punish him for his treachery.

On the second grand tour, during which the griffin flew much more rapidly than before, his tail was raised higher in the air, so that Atto, still clinging to it, was obliged to stand on the tips of his toes. The prince shouted to the griffin to lower his tail, but the latter paid no attention to him, but flew faster and faster, darting upward and downward and from one side to the other.

Now the tail was stuck perpendicularly upward, and Atto clung to it, as he would to the mast of a tossing ship. Then, without the least warning, and in the midst of a wild swoop, the tail went straight out behind, and Atto found himself hanging beneath it, his legs and arms turned about it, as if it had been a horizontal bar in a gymnasium.

Nearly frightened out of his wits, the young prince began to shout for help, and as he did so the griffin swung his tail from right to left, and sometimes dipped it downward, so that Atto's feet were higher than his head. The flights became swifter and wilder than before, and mounting high into the air, the griffin suddenly dropped downward as if he would strike the earth, but before reaching it, rose again with a great swoop and recommenced his mad gyrations above the people's heads.

During this astounding and blood-thrilling performance every breath was held and every heart beat fast. Even the flying monsters of Kobol-land had never known of anything like this. Every one was wild with admiration at Atto's amazing strength and courage. His cries had been heard, but it was supposed that he was shouting to his steed and urging him to swifter speed. But the griffin did not intend that Atto should get any credit for his performance. He understood the applause, and having thoroughly frightened the prince, he proceeded to let the public know what sort of a man this bold rider really was.

He curled up his tail so that Atto was able to scramble on his back and sit astride of him; then he sailed slowly around the arena not very far above the heads of the spectators. Atto now began to cry piteously for help. He besought the king, the queen, Lista, anybody, to stop the monster and take him down. He declared that he had not wanted to do this thing, that he had been forced into it, and if the griffin began again to rush through the air he should certainly fall to the ground and be killed. He wiped his weeping eyes with the scarf Millice had given him, and when it was thoroughly wet he threw it to the ground.

Many of the spectators pitied the prince, but more laughed at

PRINCE ATTO TAKES A RIDE WITH THE GRIFFIN.

him. The Kobol-landers were delighted ; here was a grand victory by one of themselves over a human being of high degree.

But the griffin was resolved that Atto should not even be pitied. Presently a young dragon came toward him, bearing a large banner with an inscription upon it. This the monster took in his fore-paws, and holding it high over his head, continued his slow course. The inscription, in great black letters, read as follows :

"The fellow on my back has been punished for playing false with a griffin and trying to cheat a gardener."

As nearly all the people of Tanobar and Nustyria were interested in gardening and gardeners, and as all the inhabitants of Kobol-land sympathized with griffins, a yell of derision arose from the crowd. But Atto paid little attention to this, nor did he even look upward to read the inscription. All he cared for was to get down from the griffin's back, and he continued to weep and beg and pray that some man, woman, giant, or even gnome or fairy, would take pity on him.

Now uprose Queen Millice, and as the flying monster passed near her, she cried out to him :

"Good griffin, he has had enough of punishment. I beg that you will take him to his tent and leave him there."

At these words the griffin turned, and Atto began to pour out thanks to the young queen, but she did not so much as look at him, and the griffin carried him to his tent and dumped him off at the door.

The griffin's performance was much enjoyed by those people of Tanobar who had a contempt for Nustyrians, by those Nustyrians who had a contempt for Atto, and by those Kobol-landers who had a contempt for human beings.

The entertainment of the next afternoon began with something of a totally different character from the griffin act. This was a spelling bee, and the judges were a learned man, a wizard, and the Queen of the Fairies. As Millice had done nothing so far, she thought it but right that she should enter this contest. Chamian and Lista were also among the competitors, as well as many persons attached to the courts of the two countries, and a miscellaneous lot of Kobol-landers.

The words given out by the judges were generally very odd and unusual ones, and a good deal of the spelling of the competi-

THE JUDGES OF THE GAMES.

tors was even more odd and unusual. All the afrits, gnomes, dragons, genii, and other inhabitants of Kobol-land spoke the languages of the adjoining countries. For if these strange and semi-natural creatures could not use and comprehend the speech of man, they would lose a greater part of the interest which has always attached to them, but as few of them knew anything about reading or writing their ideas of spelling were mystical and vague.

When a goat-legged satyr spelled "supersapient" as a word of two letters beginning and ending with *y*, and when a bottle-green imp, perched on the shoulders of a giant in order that he might see and be seen, spelled "gormandizer" with the figures 1, 8, 4, 3, it was plain that they knew what they wanted to spell if they did not know how to do it.

King Chamian did very well, although he failed on some five-syllabled word, but Lista spelled "euphemistic" *youphumistick*, and when the judges, seeing she was not at home in this class of words, gave her "saddle," she spelled it with one *d*, and the *e* where the *l* ought to be.

Queen Millice was by all odds the best speller on the grounds, and the audience became quite enthusiastic at her success with every word given her, no matter how hard it was, or how many had failed before her. Even "rodomontade" she spelled without an *h*, although "rhododendron" had been given out a little while before.

When Prince Atto, who had not shown himself since his griffin act, heard there was to be a spelling bee, he was anxious to take part, for he was very proud of his abilities as a speller; and feeling that he might now regain some of the reputation he had lost the day before, he ventured into the arena. He had changed his clothes and was not recognized by the greater part of the crowd, but the judges knew him and they gave him the hardest words they could think of. However, they found no fault with his spelling until he came to the word "xylophagan," and then the Queen of the Fairies cried out, "Wrong, he should spell it with a *z*."

"I beg your pardon," said the learned man, "but if I am not mistaken the word begins with an *x*, as he spelled it."

"Nonsense," exclaimed the Fairy Queen, whose face had begun to glow with indignation the moment she had perceived Atto, "you need not try to make me believe that a cowardly cheat such as that fellow understands spelling better than I do. No one can hear the word without knowing that it begins with a *z*. What say you, wizard?"

The wizard, who knew on which side his bread was buttered, replied to the Fairy Queen that he agreed with her perfectly. The learned man, with two against him, could do no more, and Atto was told to sit down.

The athletic games ended with a grand football match, in which there were hundreds of players. The contest was very exciting, and Lista became so wildly enthusiastic that she fairly scolded Chamian for not joining in this grand sport.

"Oh, if I were only a man," she cried, "I should show you how I could kick."

But Chamian did not care to take part in this game. He had begun to think more of his dignity, and therefore restrained his inclination to enter the rough-and-tumble scramble in the arena. During the applause which followed the exploits of a jet-black centaur, with a curly head and enormous hind hoofs, Chamian left Lista and went to the pavilion of Millice. He learned that she had left the arena and gone to see the last of the flower show. Joining her there, he found her in conversation with the griffin.

"Yes," the monster was saying, "you are the only person in all that crowd who had the courage to speak to me and ask me to stop tormenting that poor rascal, and in order to show you how I appreciate your brave spirit I am going to give you my prize chrysanthemum," and he thereupon presented her with the great plant covered with its fiery and sparkling flowers.

When the monster had left, Chamian and Millice walked together through the beautiful passageways, and he congratulated her on her victory at the spelling bee.

"It must be ever so much harder," he said, "to spell the words they gave you than to fence with a unicorn."

ATHLETES AT THE GAMES.

Just then they came to the cup-of-tea plant, which Chamian had not before noticed. Millice wanted some tea, and stopping, she broke off and filled two blossoms, one of which she handed to Chamian. The king sipped it, and declared that as a rule he did not care for tea, but that this was delicious.

Not far away the sorcerer stood, watching the young couple,

and as he watched, he smiled more and more. Presently he summoned his body servant.

"Graglick," he said, "measure my grin."

Taking a tape measure from his pocket, the servant obeyed.

"Master," he said, "it is nine and a half inches long."

"I thought things would turn out in that way," the sorcerer said to himself, "if they were brought together away from home."

When Millice had retired to her tent, Chamian said to the gardener:

"I wish to buy this cup-of-tea plant, and make it a present to the queen. Send it to the palace, and I will pay you your price."

That evening the exhibition was pronounced closed, and every road was covered with the visitors returning to their homes, all delighted with the success of the great show in Kobol-land.

At daybreak Lista mounted her wicked mare, and set off for home at full speed, soon outstripping her attendants, as was her custom. In the course of the morning she overtook Atto, on his elephant. He had left the Dimmer-Glade in the night, and was now reclining on his cushioned platform studying a book of logarithms. Lista pulled up her horse.

"Heigho, Miss Atto," she cried, "going home, are you, to show your papa and mamma the prize you took in the great griffin act?"

Atto turned slowly over and looked down at her.

"Where is your great prize?" he said; "I don't see him anywhere. Did you ride so fast that you left him behind you?"

"What prize do you mean?" asked Lista, sharply.

"I mean the King of Tanobar," replied Atto.

Lista turned red in the face and shook her whip at Atto, and then, too angry to say a word, she dashed away.

Two days after his return King Chamian left his apartments in the royal palace, and walked to the other end of the splendid building to visit Millice, which was a very unusual thing for him to do.

"Cousin," he said, when they were together, "do you not think it would be well if this kingdom should have but one throne, and that we both should sit upon it?"

The young queen played with her fan.

"Do you think it could be made wide enough?" she asked.

"Oh, I will see to that," he exclaimed.

"And we shall each wear the crown we inherited?" said she.

"Indeed we shall," he cried, "and you shall be doubly queen— queen as my wife, and queen as your father's child."

The eyes of Millice sparkled as she looked upon the noble and glowing face of Chamian.

"And you shall be the king that you are," she said, "and my king besides."

When it was proclaimed that Millice and Chamian were to marry, and that there was to be but one royal family in Tanobar, the joy of the people knew no bounds. But in the midst of the universal happiness the Minister of Agriculture stood shocked and downcast. He had not expected this blow—but he was a man of action, and he felt that if he made any hay at all he must do it while the sun yet shone, so he hastened to the king.

"Your majesty," said he, "as a proof of my rapturous delight on this glad day I wish to offer you the best I have—the result of my life's most earnest labors. I give to you my Cosmic Bean. It gained four first prizes at the great show, and its value is now undoubted. Take it, my king! Through you I give it to my country."

"How many plants have you?" asked the king.

"I have twenty," answered Gromline; "they are here in these pots, which my servants have brought you."

"And have you any seeds or slips besides?" inquired Chamian.

"None, your majesty," said the minister, "but there are pods there which will soon be ripe, and you will have seeds enough to spread broadcast over the kingdom."

"Very good," said Chamian. "I accept your gift."

When the king next saw Millice, he found her admiring her chrysanthemum and her cup-of-tea plant.

"I, too, have had a horticultural present," he said, and he told her of Gromline's gift of the Cosmic Bean.

"That is the plant which will make it unnecessary for people to work, is it not?" she asked.

"Yes," he said, "and I want to consult you as to what shall be done with it."

"It is my opinion," said Millice, "that if we do not wish to be king and queen of Lazyland, it will be well to utterly destroy this plant. For if no one need work, no one would work, and in the course of time we should become as cattle, and live on beans as they live on grass."

"You speak well," said the king, "and I agree with you entirely." And he ordered the twenty plants of the Cosmic Bean, pots and all, to be cast into a furnace and burned up.

Shortly after this had been done the sorcerer called on the Minister of Agriculture and found him in a very angry mood, and engaged in packing up his goods and chattels.

"I am going to leave this wretched country," said Gromline; "everything has gone wrong. Your advice about getting up the great show in Kobol-land was worse than worthless, and you ought to repay me the seventy sequins I gave you for it."

"I don't do business in that way," said the sorcerer. "I consider that the advice was worth double the money. It made you a positive benefactor to your country. In your efforts to create dissensions in the land, and by means of your universal food, to put yourself at the head of a mob of lazy people, whom you would cheat into the belief that you would allow them to live without work, you have brought together our king and queen, who otherwise might never have found out how well suited to each other they were. You have cultivated friendly relations between Tanobar and Nustyria, and above all, in endeavoring to work upon the generous feelings of the king you have put out of existence that baneful plant, which would have taken from men the incentive to the improvement of their condition ; and so I say there never was a grander success than the great show in Kobol-land."

"Away with you," cried Gromline, and went on with his packing.

SCRIBNER'S BOOKS FOR THE YOUNG.

A NEW BOOK BY MR. STOCKTON.

THE CLOCKS OF RONDAINE
AND OTHER STORIES.
By FRANK R. STOCKTON.

With 24 illustrations by E. H. BLASHFIELD, W. A. ROGERS, D. C. BEARD and others.

One Volume, square 8vo, $1.50.

The whimsical humor of Mr. Stockton's odd fancies will make his new book alike enjoyable to old and young readers. There are seven stories in the volume, in each of which some quaint conceit is elaborated with a matter-of-fact seriousness of manner that is as artistic as it is amusing in its effect. These stories include the title-tale, narrating the experiences of the girl who tried to make all the clocks in the town keep time with her own; a story in which the telephone plays the principal part; a characteristic account of the adventures of a couple on an abandoned steamship; a Christmas tale for boys, which will rank with the best of the author's work; a tricycle story with a climax both grotesque and disastrous, etc., etc. The illustrations are numerous and cleverly harmonize with the spirit of the stories

PERSONALLY CONDUCTED.

By FRANK R. STOCKTON. With 46 illustrations by JOSEPH PENNELL, ALFRED PARSONS and others. One volume, square 8vo, $2.00.

"In Frank Stockton, the boys and girls have a cicerone skilled in the art of conversation, a traveler conversant with all the curious and characteristic things of the Old World, and a story teller renowned for the audacity of his stories."—*Critic.*

STOCKTON'S OTHER BOOKS.

The Story of Viteau. With 16 full-page illustrations by R. B. BIRCH. 12mo, extra cloth, $1.50.
"It is as romantic and absorbing as any boy could wish for, full of adventure and daring, and yet told in excellent spirit and with a true literary instinct."—*Christian Union.*

A Jolly Fellowship. With 20 illustrations. 12mo, $1.50.
"We can think of no book published the present season which will more delight the wide-awake, adventure-loving boy. It is, to borrow the adjective from the title, just 'jolly.'"—*Boston Transcript.*

The Floating Prince and other Fairy Tales. With illustrations. Square 8vo, $1.50.
"These tales are full of the quaintest conceits and the oddest fancies, and the strange adventures in which the different characters engage are just the kind to excite the intense interest of children."—*Philadelphia Bulletin.*

The Ting-A-Ling Tales. With numerous illustrations. 12mo, $1.00.
"It would be difficult to find anything more dainty, fanciful and humorous than these tales of magic, faries, dwarfs and giants. There is a vein of satire in them too which adult readers will enjoy."—*N. Y. Herald.*

Roundabout Rambles in Lands of Fact and Fiction. With 200 illustrations. Square 8vo, $1.50.

Tales Out of School. With nearly 200 illustrations. Square 8vo, $1.50.
"The volumes are profusely illustrated and contain the most entertaining sketches in Mr. Stockton's most entertaining manner."—*Christian Union.*

SCRIBNER'S BOOKS FOR THE YOUNG.

NEW BOOKS BY G. A. HENTY.

For the Season of 1892-93 Mr. Henty adds to his list of fascinating stories of adventure for boys three new books—BERIC THE BRITON; A STORY OF THE ROMAN INVASION; IN GREEK WATERS; A STORY OF THE GRECIAN WAR OF INDEPENDENCE; and, CONDEMNED AS A NIHILIST; A STORY OF ESCAPE FROM SIBERIA.

Mr. Henty's stories are not only thrilling tales of adventure, but are graphic and accurate pictures of the people and the times, and are thus instructive as well as entertaining.

"*Among writers of stories of adventure he stands in the very first rank.*"—ACADEMY.
"*Mr. Henty is one of the best of story tellers for young people.*"—SPECTATOR.

BERIC THE BRITON:

A STORY OF THE ROMAN INVASION. By G. A. HENTY. With 12 full-page illustrations by W. PARKINSON. Crown 8vo, handsomely bound, olivine edges, $1.50.

This story deals with the invasion of Britain by the Roman legionaries. Beric, who is a boy chief of a British tribe, takes a prominent part in the insurrection under Boadicea; and after the defeat of that heroic queen (in A. D. 62) he continues the struggle in the fen-country. Ultimately after many exciting adventures Beric is defeated and is carried captive to Rome, where he becomes a gladiator. A thrilling chapter is the account of his saving a Christain maid by slaying a lion in the arena, his reward being that he is made the personal protector of the Emperor Nero. Finally he escapes and, returning to Britain, becomes a wise ruler of his own people.

IN GREEK WATERS:

A STORY OF THE GRECIAN WAR OF INDEPENDENCE (1821-1827). By G. A. HENTY. With 12 full-page illustrations by W. S. STACEY, and a map. Crown 8vo, handsomely bound, olivine edges, $1.50.

A large part of this story deals with the revolt of the Greeks, in 1821, against Turkish oppression. Mr. Beveridge and his son Horace, like most Englishmen at that time, are stirred with enthusiasm for the down-trodden nation. So they fit out a privateer, load it with military stores, and set sail for Greece to assist the insurgents. On their arrival, however, they find that the leaders of the insurrection are a cowardly, thieving, blood-thirsty crew. So they resolve to hold aloof from politics, and devote themselves to assisting the victims of war on both sides. The story is full of stirring adventure, and will delight the boy who loves the sea and the hazards of seafaring.

CONDEMNED AS A NIHILIST:

A STORY OF ESCAPE FROM SIBERIA. By G. A. HENTY. With 8 full-page illustrations by WALTER PAGET. Crown 8vo, handsomely bound, olivine edges, $1.50.

Godfrey Bullen, the hero of this story, an English boy resident in St. Petersburg, becomes involved in a political plot, and is exiled to a convict settlement in Northern Siberia. His first attempt to escape is unsuccessful, and he is put at work in the mines at Kara. He again escapes; walks 800 miles till he reaches the Angara River; buys a canoe and sails down the Siberian rivers for a thousand miles; coasts along the Arctic shores of Russia, and at last after many exciting adventures with bears, wolves, and hostile Samoyedes, he reaches Norway, and thence home after a perilous journey which lasts nearly two years.

SCRIBNER'S BOOKS FOR THE YOUNG.

REDSKIN AND COWBOY.

A Tale of the Western Plains. By G. A. HENTY. With 12 full-page illustrations by ALFRED PEARSE. Crown 8vo, handsomely bound, olivine edges, $1.50.

"Mr. Henty seems to be the lineal descendant of Mayne Reid in the production of exciting stories of adventure. This book is said to be founded on the experiences of a young English friend of the author, and though it is full of hairbreadth escapes, none of the incidents are improbable. It is needless to say that the English lad's adventures are well told."—*San Francisco Chronicle*.

THE DASH FOR KHARTOUM.

A Tale of the Nile Expedition. By G. A. HENTY. With 10 full-page illustrations by JOHN SCHÖNBERG and J. NASH, and 4 Plans. Crown 8vo, handsomely bound, olivine edges, $1.50.

"Mr. Henty's story of the Nile expedition and of the attempt to rescue General Gordon, is brought out with much spirit and skill. There were deeds of daring done in that campaign as brave as any that throw a lustre on the pages of English history. In freshness of treatment and variety of incident the story is fit to rank with anything from the pen of Captain Mayne Reid."—*Philadelphia Record*.

REPELLING THE TURKISH BOARDERS.

HELD FAST FOR ENGLAND.

A Tale of the Siege of Gibraltar. By G. A. HENTY. With 8 full-page illustrations by GORDON BROWNE. Crown 8vo, handsomely bound, olivine edges, $1.50.

"It is an historical novel, the siege of Gibraltar by the combined forces of France and Spain, in the latter part of the eighteenth century, being the foundation on which Mr. Henty's clever fiction rests. It is a story of pluck and adventure on sea and land."—*Newark Advertiser*.

"The story, for those who care for battle and adventure by land or sea in the last century, will be found very interesting."—*N. Y. Commercial Advertiser*.

SCRIBNER'S BOOKS FOR THE YOUNG.

THE THIRSTY SWORD.

A STORY OF THE NORSE INVASION OF SCOTLAND (1262-65).
By ROBERT LEIGHTON.

With 8 full-page illustrations by ALFRED PEARSE, and a map.

One volume, crown 8vo, - - $1.50.

"AASTA GRIPPED HER SWORD AND LEAPT UPON RODERIC."

In this story of *The Thirsty Sword* and the vengeance which it accomplishes, there is found much of the simple directness and tragic strength of the old Scandinavian Sagas. It is laid in that period of Scottish history which ended with the famous battle of Largs; and it tells how Roderic MacAlpin, the sea rover, came to the Isle of Bute; how he slew his brother, Earl Hamish, in Rothesay Castle; how Alpin, the earl's eldest son, challenged his uncle to ordeal by battle, and was likewise slain; how young Kenric now became King of Bute, and vowed vengeance against the slayer of his brother and father; and finally it tells how this vow was kept when Kenric and the murderous sea rover met at midnight on Garroch Head, and ended their feud in one last great fight.

THE PILOTS OF POMONA.

A STORY OF THE ORKNEY ISLANDS. By ROBERT LEIGHTON. With 8 full-page illustrations by JOHN LEIGHTON. One volume, crown 8vo, $1.50.

"It is finely written and full of adventure, and the characters stand out clearly upon the canvas upon which they are drawn."—*Brooklyn Citizen.*

THREE BOOKS BY HJALMAR H. BOYESEN.

BOYHOOD IN NORWAY.	AGAINST HEAVY ODDS.	THE MODERN VIKINGS.
Nine Stories of Deeds of the Sons of the Vikings. With 8 illustrations. 12mo, $1.50	A Tale of Norse Heroism. With 13 full-page illustrations by W. L. TAYLOR. 12mo, $1.00.	Stories of Life and Sport in the Norseland. With many full-page illustrations. 12mo. *New and cheaper edition*, $1.50.

SCRIBNER'S BOOKS FOR THE YOUNG.

OTTO OF THE SILVER HAND.
WRITTEN AND ILLUSTRATED BY HOWARD PYLE.
With Twenty-five Full-Page and many other Illustrations.

One volume, royal 8vo, half leather, - - - - - - - $2.00

"The scene of the story is mediæval Germany in the time of feuds and robber barons and romance. The kidnapping of Otto, his adventures among rough soldiers, and his daring rescue, make up a spirited and thrilling story. The drawings are in keeping with the text, and in mechanical and artistic qualities as well as in literary execution the book must be greeted as one of the very best juveniles of the year, quite worthy to succeed to the remarkable popularity of Mr. Pyle's 'Robin Hood.'"—*Christian Union.*

"Told with vividness and uncommon spirit."
—*Troy Press.*
"Far above the common run of juvenile tales."
—*Pittsburg Post.*
"Handsome and attractive in every respect."
—*New York Herald.*

"An addition of the highest character to juvenile literature."—*Boston Times.*
"The decorative head and tail pieces, etc., add much to the embellishment and rich holiday appearance of the book."—*Portland Argus.*
"Far above the average quality of stories for the young. Mr. Pyle is seen in his most brilliant light in both the text and illustrations. The volume is a handsome specimen of a holiday book."—*Boston Saturday Gazette.*

THE MERRY ADVENTURES OF ROBIN HOOD
OF GREAT RENOWN IN NOTTINGHAMSHIRE.
WRITTEN AND ELABORATELY ILLUSTRATED BY HOWARD PYLE.

One volume, royal 8vo, - - - - - - - - - $3.00

"A superb book."—*Chicago Inter-Ocean.*
"A very original work."—*Boston Post.*
"A captivating book."—*London Daily News.*
"An excellent piece of literary, artistic and mechanical work."—*Louisville Commercial.*
"This superb book is unquestionably the most original and elaborate ever produced by any American artist. Mr. Pyle has told, with pencil and pen, the complete and consecutive story of Robin Hood and his merry men in

their haunts in Sherwood Forest, gathered from the old ballads and legends. Mr Pyle's admirable illustrations are strewn profusely through the book."—*Boston Transcript.*

SCRIBNER'S BOOKS FOR THE YOUNG.

BRIC-A-BRAC STORIES.
BY MRS. BURTON HARRISON.

Specimen Illustration, reduced.

With 24 full-page Illustrations by Walter Crane.

One volume, 12mo, new and cheaper edition, $1.50.

"When the little boy, for whose benefit the various articles of bric-a-brac in his father's drawing-room relate stories appropriate to their several native countries, exclaims, at the conclusion of one of them: 'I almost think there can't be a better one than that!' the reader, of whatever age, will probably feel inclined to agree with him. Upon the whole, it is to be wished that every boy and girl in America, or anywhere else, might become intimately acquainted with the contents of this book. There is more virtue in one of these stories than in the entire library of modern juvenile literature."—*Julian Hawthorne.*

THE OLD-FASHIONED FAIRY BOOK.
BY MRS. BURTON HARRISON.
With many Quaint Illustrations by Miss Rosina Emmet.

One volume, square 16mo, - - - - - - - $1.25.

"The little ones, who so willingly go back with us to 'Jack the Giant Killer,' 'Bluebeard,' and the kindred stories of our childhood, will gladly welcome Mrs. Burton Harrison's 'Old-Fashioned Fairy Tales,' where the giant, the dwarf, the fairy, the wicked princess, the ogre, the metamorphosed prince, and all the heroes of that line come into play and action. The graceful pencil of Miss Rosina Emmet has given a pictorial interest to the book."—*Frank R. Stockton.*

LITTLE PEOPLE:
And Their Homes in Meadows, Woods and Waters.
BY STELLA LOUISE HOOK.
Beautifully Illustrated by Dan Beard and Harry Beard.

One volume, square 8vo, - - - - $1.50.

"A beautifully illustrated volume for young people, in which the habits, humors, and eccentricities of insects are delightfully described. The secrets and charms of insect-land are laid open by her vivacious pen, and the astonishing insects are described in a manner that makes them personal acquaintances."
—*Cambridge Tribune.*

SCRIBNER'S BOOKS FOR THE YOUNG.

A NEW VOLUME OF STORIES BY MR. PAGE.

AMONG THE CAMPS;
OR, YOUNG PEOPLE'S STORIES OF THE WAR.
BY THOMAS NELSON PAGE.

With Eight full-page Illustrations by W. L. Sheppard and others.

One volume, square 8vo, uniform with "Two Little Confederates," $1.50.

TITLES.—A CAPTURED SANTA CLAUS. KITTYKIN, AND THE PART SHE PLAYED IN THE WAR. NANCY PANSY. JACK AND JAKE.

The popularity of Mr. Page's charming story of the "Two Little Confederates" was and is so great—12,000 copies of the book having been sold—that a new book by the same author is of unusual interest for young readers. The scenes of these fresh stories of the war are laid in Virginia—a field in which Mr. Page is unrivaled—and they are told with all the vivacity, feeling and humor that has made the author's earlier story such delightful reading. They are interesting, not only as stories which will entertain young readers, but as accurate pictures of phases of life in Virginia during the war.

TWO LITTLE CONFEDERATES.
BY THOMAS NELSON PAGE.

With Eight full-page Illustrations by E. W. Kemble and A. C. Redwood.

One volume, square 8vo, — — — — *$1.50.*

"Most delightful."—*New York Times.*

"There is both humor and pathos in the book, and its literary qualities are as high as any book for young folks printed since 'Little Lord Fauntleroy.'"—*Christian Union.*

"The story is beautifully told, fun and pathos being equally mingled in its ingenious threads. The book is a handsome octavo and is fully illustrated."—*Newark Advertiser.*

"It tells the story of two Virginia lads left at home on a plantation while the men went to fight. The youngsters have many adventures, serious and humorous, and get into trouble and out of it again. The story abounds in stirring incidents, and gives a very picturesque view of home life in Virginia during the rebellion. It is *an admirable juvenile book*, teaching an excellent moral of self-reliance."—*The Boston Saturday Gazette.*

SCRIBNER'S BOOKS FOR THE YOUNG.

A NEW SERIES FOR BOYS.

Bound in uniform style and sold at $1.25 each.

THE BOY SETTLERS.
A STORY OF EARLY TIMES IN KANSAS.

BY NOAH BROOKS.

With Sixteen full-page Illustrations by W. A. Rogers.

One volume, 12mo, - - $1.25.

In "The Boy Settlers" Noah Brooks has written a companion volume to his popular "Boy Emigrants," a new and cheaper edition of which is issued simultaneously. "The Boy Settlers" is a story of adventure and incident in Kansas in the exciting days when that State was the battle ground between the border ruffians and the emigrants from the North over the slavery question.

"It is full of incident and adventure, in a style well fitted not only to captivate the young, but also to beguile the maturer reader into losing himself for a while in the fresh stirring life of a new settlement."
—*N. Y. Journal of Commerce.*

"SURE ENOUGH, THERE THEY WERE, TWENTY-FIVE OR THIRTY INDIANS."
Reduced from "The Boy Settlers."

THE BOY EMIGRANTS.

BY NOAH BROOKS.

With Illustrations by T. Moran and W. L. Sheppard. 12mo, $1.25.

"It is one of the best boy's stories we have ever read. There is nothing morbid or unhealthy about it. His heroes are thorough boys, with all the faults of their age."—*The Christian at Work.*

A NEW MEXICO DAVID.
AND OTHER STORIES AND SKETCHES OF THE SOUTHWEST.

BY CHARLES F. LUMMIS.

With Eight full-page Illustrations. One volume, 12mo, $1.25.

These eighteen stories and sketches are true pictures of the life of the wonderful and almost unknown Southwest, and are based upon the author's acquaintance with its quaint peoples, its weird customs, and its dangers, made during a long residence among the Indians and Mexicans. The stories relate to old legends, and to the Indians, gold hunters and cowboys of the Southwest, and are of absorbing interest.

SCRIBNER'S BOOKS FOR THE YOUNG.

MARVELS OF ANIMAL LIFE SERIES.

By CHARLES F. HOLDER. Three volumes, 8vo, each profusely illustrated. Singly, $1.75. The Set, $5.00.

THE IVORY KING.

A Popular History of the Elephant and its Allies. With Twenty-four full-page Illustrations, $1.75.

"The author also talks in a lively and pleasant way about white elephants, rogue elephants, baby elephants, trick elephants, of the elephant in war, pageantry, sports, and games. A charming accession to books for young people."—*The Chicago Interior.*

MARVELS OF ANIMAL LIFE.

With Twenty-four full-page Illustrations, $1.75.

"Mr. Holder combines his description of these odd creatures with stories of his own adventures in pursuit of them in many parts of the world. These are told with much spirit and humor, and add greatly to the fascination of the book."—*The Worcester Spy.*

LIVING LIGHTS.

A Popular Account of Phosphorescent Animals and Vegetables. With Twenty-seven full-page Illustrations, $1.75.

"Nothing could be better adapted to interest young people in natural history."—*Philadelphia Record.*

THE BOY'S LIBRARY OF LEGEND AND CHIVALRY.

Edited by SIDNEY LANIER, and richly illustrated by FREDERICKS, BENSELL, and KAPPES. Four volumes, cloth, uniform binding, price per set, $7.00. Sold separately, price per volume, $2.00.

Mr. Lanier's books present to boy readers the old English classics of history and legend in an attractive form. While they are stories of action and stirring incident, they teach those lessons which manly, honest boys ought to learn.

THE BOY'S KING ARTHUR.

THE BOY'S FROISSART.

THE BOY'S PERCY.

THE KNIGHTLY LEGENDS OF WALES.

"Amid all the strange and fanciful scenery of these stories, character and ideals of character remain at the simplest and purest. The romantic history transpires in the healthy atmosphere of the open air on the green turf beneath the open sky."—*The Independent.*

SCRIBNER'S BOOKS FOR THE YOUNG.

CHILDREN'S STORIES IN ENGLISH LITERATURE.

TALIESIN TO SHAKESPEARE—SHAKESPEARE TO TENNYSON.

BY HENRIETTA CHRISTIAN WRIGHT.

Two volumes, 12mo, each, - - - - $1.25

"The first volume of Miss Wright's 'Children's Stories in English Literature' took the young reader down to Shakespeare; the new volume continues the bright and entertaining narrative 'From Shakespeare to Tennyson,' thus completing a work upon the first part of which the highest praise has been bestowed.

"The study of our literature is made fascinating for Miss Wright's readers by the skilful use she makes of the biographical glimpses she gives of each author, and by the excellent pictures she draws of the life of which they were contemporaries. She is a reliable guide who conveys much charming information."—*Cambridge Tribune.*

"It is indeed a vivid history of the people as well as a story of their literature; and, brief as it is, the author has so deftly seized on all the salient points, that the child who has read this book will be more thoroughly acquainted than many a student of history with the life and thought of the centuries over which the work reaches."—*The Evangelist.*

BY THE SAME AUTHOR.

CHILDREN'S STORIES

OF THE GREAT SCIENTISTS.

With numerous Portraits.   12mo, $1.25

"The author has succeeded in making her pen pictures of the great scientists as graphic as the excellent portraits that illustrate the work. Around each name she has picturesquely grouped the essential features of scientific achievement."—*Brooklyn Times.*

OF AMERICAN PROGRESS.

Illustrated.   12mo, $1.25

"Miss Wright is favorably known by her volume of well-told 'Stories in American History,' and her 'Stories of American Progress' is equally worthy of commendation. Taken together they present a series of pictures of great graphic interest. The illustrations are excellent."—*The Nation.*

IN AMERICAN HISTORY.

Illustrated.   12mo, $1.25

"A most delightful and instructive collection of historical events, told in a simple and pleasant manner. Almost every occurrence in the gradual development of our country is woven into an attractive story for young people."—*San Francisco Evening Post.*

SCRIBNER'S BOOKS FOR THE YOUNG.

THE BOY'S LIBRARY OF PLUCK AND ACTION.

Four volumes, 12mo, in a box, illustrated, - - - - - **$5.00**
Sold separately, price per volume, - - - - - - **1.50**

A JOLLY FELLOWSHIP.
BY FRANK R. STOCKTON.

HANS BRINKER;
OR, THE SILVER SKATES.
A Story of Life in Holland.
BY MRS. MARY MAPES DODGE.

THE BOY EMIGRANTS.
BY NOAH BROOKS.

PHAETON ROGERS.
BY ROSSITER JOHNSON.

In the "*Boy's Library of Pluck and Action,*" the design was to bring together the representative and most popular books of four of the best known writers for young people. The volumes are beautifully illustrated and uniformly bound in a most attractive form.

ILLUSTRATED LIBRARY OF TRAVEL.
BY BAYARD TAYLOR.

Per set, six volumes, 12mo, $6.00.   **Each with many illustrations.**
Sold separately, per volume, - - **$1.25.**

JAPAN IN OUR DAY.
TRAVELS IN ARABIA.
TRAVELS IN SOUTH AFRICA.
CENTRAL ASIA.
THE LAKE REGION OF CENTRAL AFRICA.
SIAM, THE LAND OF THE WHITE ELEPHANT.

Each volume is complete in itself, and contains, first, a brief preliminary sketch of the country to which it is devoted, next, such an outline of previous explorations as may be necessary to explain what has been achieved by later ones; and finally, a condensation of one or more of the most important narratives of recent travel, accompanied with illustrations of the scenery, architecture, and life of the races drawn only from the most authentic sources.

"Authenticated accounts of countries, peoples, modes of living and being, curiosities in natural history, and personal adventure in travels and explorations, suggest a rich fund of solid instruction combined with delightful entertainment. The editorship by one of the most observant and well-travelled men of modern times, at once secures the high character of the 'Library' in every particular."—*The Sunday School Times.*

SCRIBNER'S BOOKS FOR THE YOUNG.

STORIES FOR BOYS.

BY RICHARD HARDING DAVIS.

With six full-page Illustrations. One volume, 12mo. - - $1.00.

CONTENTS.—THE REPORTER WHO MADE HIMSELF KING. MIDSUMMER PIRATES. RICHARD CARR'S BABY; A FOOTBALL STORY. THE GREAT TRI-CLUB TENNIS TOURNAMENT. THE JUMP AT COREY'S SLIP. THE VAN BIBBER BASEBALL CLUB. THE STORY OF A JOCKEY.

"THE WAVE SWEPT BY HER AND THE DEFEATED CREW SALUTED THE VICTORS WITH CHEERS."

In freshness of theme and originality of treatment, these boys' stories are characteristic of the popular author of "Gallegher," who is himself an expert in all manly sports. Mr. Davis puts an immense amount of snap and dash into these exciting stories of the sports that all wide-awake, healthy boys are interested in, with just a touch of pathos here and there to emphasize some manly trait in his young heroes of the field and the water. Every boy will find them rattling good stories.

SCRIBNER'S BOOKS FOR THE YOUNG.

STANLEY'S GREAT AFRICAN STORY FOR BOYS.

MY KALULU.

PRINCE, KING AND SLAVE. A STORY OF CENTRAL AFRICA.
BY HENRY M. STANLEY.

One volume, 12mo, New Edition, with many Illustrations, $1.50.

Mr. Stanley's African romance for boys is based upon knowledge acquired during his journey in search of Dr. Livingstone, which began in 1871 and ended in 1872. It is a fascinating story of strange scenes, incidents and adventures among the tribes of Central Africa, and of encounters with the wild animals that make their home there.

"A fresh, breezy, stirring story for youths, interesting in itself and full of information regarding life in the interior of the continent in which its scenes are laid."—*The New York Times.*

"If the young reader is fond of strange adventures, he will find enough in this volume to delight him all winter, and he will be hard to please who is not charmed by its graphic pages."—*Boston Journal.*

ADVENTURES OF CAPTAIN MAGO;

Or, A Phœnician Expedition, B. C. 1000. By LÉON CAHUN. With 73 Illustrations. New Edition, $1.50.

A narrative of strange and perilous adventures by land and sea, and presenting a vivid and accurate picture of the world as it was known to the Phœnician navigators and travelers 1000 years before the Christian era.

A TALE OF THE INDIAN MUTINY;

Or, The Serpent-Charmer. By LOUIS ROUSSELET. New Edition, Fully Illustrated. 12mo, $1.50.

"The book, the plot of which appears to be founded on fact, is rather a boy's book than a novel, and is filled with an uninterrupted series of wild adventures, told in an agreeable and interesting way."
—*The Nation.*

WILD MEN AND WILD BEASTS; OR, SCENES IN CAMP AND JUNGLE.

BY LIEUT.-COL. GORDON CUMMING.

New Edition, Illustrated, - - One Volume, 12mo, $1.50.

The author of this book is famous for his hunting exploits in Africa and in Asia. His narrative has an autobiographical basis and contians some of the most marvelous stories of adventure ever published. Col. Gordon Cumming's accounts of his various expeditions are records of bravery and endurance seldom paralleled; and the tales of bloodshed are alleviated by pleasant anecdote—the humors of the camp and chase.

SCRIBNER'S BOOKS FOR THE YOUNG.

TWO BOOKS FOR BOYS AND GIRLS.

Mr. Beard has added sixty new drawings to his "American Boy's Handy Book," to illustrate the new games, sports, and mechanical contrivances which he has incorporated in this latest edition. The Misses Beard's companion volume, "The American Girl's Handy Book," is reduced in price, all the features being retained. Both are profusely illustrated with hundreds of pictures and designs, and in their new dress will be prime favorites with holiday buyers.

THE AMERICAN BOY'S HANDY BOOK;
OR, WHAT TO DO AND HOW TO DO IT.
BY DANIEL C. BEARD.

With over 360 Illustrations by the Author.

One volume, square 8vo, - - - $2.00

"The book has this great advantage over its predecessors, that most of the games, tricks, and other amusements described in it are new. It treats of sports adapted to all seasons of the year; it is practical, and it is well illustrated."—*The New York Tribune.*

"It tells boys how to make all kinds of things—boats, traps, toys, puzzles, aquariums, fishing tackle; how to tie knots, splice ropes, to make bird-calls, sleds, blow-guns, balloons; how to rear wild birds, to train dogs, and do the thousand and one things that boys take delight in. The book is illustrated in such a way that no mistake can be made."—*The Indianapolis Journal.*

THE AMERICAN GIRL'S HANDY BOOK;
OR, HOW TO AMUSE YOURSELF AND OTHERS.
BY LENA AND ADELIA B. BEARD.

With over 500 Illustrations by the Authors.

One volume, square 8vo, - - - - $2.00

LOUISA M. ALCOTT WROTE:

"I have put it in my list of good and useful books for young people, as I have many requests for advice from my little friends and their anxious mothers. I am most happy to commend your very ingenious and entertaining book."

GRACE GREENWOOD WROTE:

"It is a treasure which, once possessed, no practical girl would willingly part with. It is an invaluable aid in making a home attractive, comfortable, artistic and refined. The book preaches the gospel of cheerfulness, industry, economy and comfort."

SCRIBNER'S BOOKS FOR THE YOUNG.

TWO JUVENILES.—BY EDWARD EGGLESTON.

THE HOOSIER SCHOOL-BOY.
One volume, 12mo. With full-page Illustrations, - - - $1.00.

"NOT THERE, NOT THERE, MY CHILD!"

Mr. Eggleston is one of the very few American writers who have succeeded in giving to their work a genuine savor of the soil, a distinctively American Character. The scene of his stories is the *Western Reserve*, and the characters are types of the early part of this century, in the territory now comprised in Indiana and Ohio. *The Hoosier Schoolboy* depicts some characteristics of boy life, years ago, on the Ohio, characteristics, however, that were not peculiar to the section only. The story presents a vivid and interesting picture of the difficulties which in those days beset the path of a youth aspiring for an education.

"Nobody has pictured boy-life with greater power or more fidelity than Mr. Eggleston. This story is one of his best—it should be in the hands of every boy."—*Hartford Times.*

QUEER STORIES FOR BOYS AND GIRLS.
One volume, 12mo, - - - - - - - - - - - $1.00.

This is a book of such stories as all boys and girls like to tell and to hear, and yet they contain as much wisdom and as many lessons of good conduct, of noble bearing and of self-respecting independence, as might be contained in volumes of sermons and reams of "good advice," that would not penetrate skin deep, nor remain five minutes in the memory of the young people who were aimed at.

SCRIBNER'S BOOKS FOR THE YOUNG.

Mrs. Burnett's Four Famous Juveniles
UNIFORM IN STYLE AND ILLUSTRATED BY R. B. BIRCH

A NEW BOOK JUST ISSUED
GIOVANNI AND THE OTHER

CHILDREN WHO HAVE MADE STORIES. By FRANCES HODGSON BURNETT. With nine full-page illustrations by REGINALD B. BIRCH. One volume, square 8vo, $1.50.

In this new volume there is a certain unity growing out of the fact that the tales, with one or two exceptions, are about little people whom Mrs. Burnett has known, an autobiographic interest thereby attaching to the charming portraits of child life. Four of the stories are about little Italian waifs who crept into the author's heart; two are of incidents in the lives of Mrs. Burnett's own boys, and the others are varied in subject. They all reveal that magic charm in the delineation of child life, the secret of which Mrs. Burnett alone seems to possess. The illustrations are unusually attractive and fully sustain Mr. Birch's reputation as a portrayer of Mrs. Burnett's little heroes and heroines.

LITTLE SAINT ELIZABETH

AND OTHER STORIES. With 12 new full-page drawings by REGINALD B. BIRCH. One volume, square 8vo, $1.50.

FROM SUSAN COOLIDGE:

"The pretty tale from which the book borrows its name has for its heroine a little French girl brought up in an old chateau in Normandy, by an aunt who is a recluse and *dévote*. A child of this type, transplanted suddenly while still in childhood to the realistic atmosphere of prosperous New York, must inevitably have much to suffer. She is puzzled; she is lonely; she has no one to direct her conscience. The quaint little figure, blindly trying to guess the riddle of duty under these unfamiliar conditions, is pathetic, and Mrs. Burnett touches it in with delicate strokes. The stories are prettily illustrated by Birch."

LITTLE LORD FAUNTLEROY

Beautifully illustrated by REGINALD B. BIRCH. One volume, square 8vo, $2.00.

FROM LOUISA M. ALCOTT:

"In 'Little Lord Fauntleroy' we gain another charming child to add to our gallery of juvenile heroes and heroines; one who teaches a great lesson with such truth and sweetness that we part with him with real regret when the episode is over."

SARA CREWE:

OR, WHAT HAPPENED AT MISS MINCHIN'S. Richly and fully illustrated by R. B. BIRCH. One volume square 8vo, $1.00.

FROM LOUISE CHANDLER MOULTON:

"Everybody was in love with 'Little Lord Fauntleroy,' and I think all the world and the rest of mankind will be in love with 'Sara Crewe.' I wish every girl in America could read it."

www.ingramcontent.com/pod-product-compliance
Lightning Source LLC
Chambersburg PA
CBHW020843160426
43192CB00007B/768